Personal Evolution

Other Hazelden publications by Veronica Ray

A Moment to Reflect on Codependency
  Accepting Ourselves
  Letting Go
  Living Our Own Lives
  Setting Boundaries

A Moment to Reflect on Self-Esteem
  I Can Make a Difference
  I Have Choices
  I Know My Self
  I'm Good Enough

A Moment to Reflect on Spirituality
  Giving
  Our Higher Power
  Receiving
  Serenity

Choosing Happiness: The Art of Living Unconditionally

Communicating with Love

Design for Growth: Twelve Steps for Adult Children

Green Spirituality: Reflections on Belonging to a World
  Beyond Myself

Other People's Successes: Moving Beyond Envy and
  Jealousy

Our Beliefs about Money: Exploring the Role of Money
  in Our Lives

Striking a Balance: How to Care without Caretaking

Personal Evolution

The Art of Living with Purpose

Veronica Ray

Hazelden Educational Materials
Center City, Minnesota 55012-0176

Editor's note
Hazelden Educational Materials offers a variety of information on chemical dependency and related areas. Our publications do not necessarily represent Hazelden's programs, nor do they officially speak for any Twelve Step organization.

The stories in this book are about real people. All names have been changed to protect their anonymity.

Contents

Contents

Acknowledgments

I am deeply grateful to Judy Delaney, Rebecca Post, and everyone at Hazelden Educational Materials; to my husband and daughter; and to all the other "teachers" from whom I have learned to find meaning and purpose in life.

Our Search for Meaning

*Man's search for meaning is the primary
motivation in his life.*

—VIKTOR FRANKL

What's life for? Why do things happen the way they do? How should we live? Why does it seem so difficult? What does it all *mean?* These are the profound questions we all ask ourselves at some time in our lives. We look to our families, religions, Twelve Step programs, governments, ethnic heritage, and schools for answers. We search in literature, art, science, philosophy, and politics. We want the meaning of life spelled out for us in a nice, neat package we can accept and understand.

After all, if the things of life have no meaning, why bother? Why suffer through the difficulties of growth and learning? Why work at our relationships and accept all the things we can't change? We search for meaning all the time, in everything we do. When we find or create it, our work can be joyful, and even our suffering can be elevated beyond mere tolerance to *purpose.* As Viktor Frankl writes in his book *Man's Search for Meaning,* "Suffering ceases to be suffering at the moment it finds a meaning."

I don't profess to have all the answers to life's hard questions for you. The purpose of this book is not for me to tell you *my* answers, but rather to help you discover your own and, just maybe, to find some that can help bring us all together. By examining the stories we grew up with and created for ourselves, we can begin seeing the worldview we've developed. I'll call this worldview our "mythology" in this book, but I'm not talking about stories of gods and goddesses or heroes and demons. I'm talking about systems of thinking about ourselves, others, the world, and life. They can be found everywhere from our own attitudes and behaviors to our literature, advertising, television programs, and corporate structures. They represent our *paradigms,* or worldviews.

These mythologies provide the framework for specific points of view. For example, the United States Constitution expresses a mythology of democracy upon which America's government has been based (however imperfectly) for over two hundred years. When old laws and practices are challenged or new ones proposed, we use the Constitution to judge them. It is America's unique manifesto or *mythology.*

"Myths," as I'm using the word here, aren't false beliefs or superstitions. Human beings are symbolic thinkers and communicators. We create and need symbols to understand our world and everything in it. We use symbols—such as pictures, language, sounds, and gestures, as well as stories, myths, and metaphors—to express ourselves. Symbols are the way we communicate with ourselves and each other. They are *bridges*— tools for connecting and communicating.

THE WAY WE THINK

Metaphors are not only fancy literary devices to use language artistically. They are the way we think, every day, all the time. Don't we all say that the sun *rises* and *sets,* even though we know it's the earth turning on its axis that produces alternating light and darkness? Doesn't everyone understand what it means to have a *broken heart* or to do a little *arm twisting* to get something we want?

We use metaphors to describe everything we think, feel, see, hear, know, and imagine. We *burn* with anger or desire and *fall* in love, asleep, and into debt or depression. We *open doors and windows* of opportunity, take the *road to recovery,* and are *reborn.* We are *thrown off balance, stay the course, lay the groundwork,* and defend arguments that *won't hold water.* Even our wars produce such euphemisms as "Desert Storm," "friendly fire," and "peacekeeping forces."

Metaphors can help us understand complicated or intangible concepts and relate new ideas to ones we're already familiar with. For example, the Buddha said, "Life is suffering." And in his book *The Road Less Traveled,* M. Scott Peck's opening sentence reads, "Life is difficult." But if I say to you, "Even in a bed of roses, there are always thorns," you are given a vivid image of what I'm talking about. Words like "suffering" and "difficult" are vague and may be interpreted differently by different people, but a bed of roses is a very specific visual image. Metaphors provide such clear mental pictures for us.

Ethical Dilemmas

Parables are stories with a moral, a lesson we can apply to a variety of situations in life. They're often taught to us by our parents, churches, or schools. From *Aesop's Fables* to religious scriptures, these parables teach us values, ethics, and how to behave in social contexts. They set up fictional precedents for us to follow and illustrate ethical dilemmas we're all likely to face in some form. They enlighten us while entertaining us.

The entertainment value of parables and fables is important. We remember the Tortoise and the Hare, the Lion and the Mouse, and the Prodigal Son more vividly than any lectures we may have heard about perseverance, kindness, or forgiveness. If someone is labeled a "Midas" or "Scrooge," we know exactly what that means. The story form is useful for understanding and remembering abstract ideas.

We may also create some of our own personal parables from our life. A childhood experience of betrayal by an important adult may become a parable for us, with the moral "Don't trust (men, women, teachers, adults, or whoever)." This lesson may stay with us long after the incident fades from our conscious memory. The morals or lessons of the parables we've learned over the years guide our behavior in many ways.

Ways of Understanding

Myths, metaphors, and parables are our ways of understanding the world, people, and ourselves. They can serve us well, helping us to make sense of our lives, find *meaning,* and communicate with others from

4

a common worldview. But sometimes the myths, metaphors, and parables no longer serve us. We may outgrow them as we change and the world changes around us. Times of crisis—such as a divorce, the death of a loved one, or recovery from an addiction—often mark the need to reevaluate our guiding beliefs. Personal growth involves reexamination of all our beliefs and the symbols we use to represent them.

Conflicts

Sometimes we run into conflicts with other people's guiding belief systems. Our differing personal meanings can make communication and harmony difficult to achieve. For example, a married couple is likely to argue about money if one partner's perspective requires thrift, saving, and sacrifice, while the other's calls for a more relaxed attitude toward spending.

We may also encounter conflicts between our own worldview and that of social groups in which we find ourselves—in business, religion, or politics, for example. Our personal ethics may prohibit lying, while our success in business seems to depend on it. Our religion may teach peace and nonviolence, while our government wants us to go to war. Political leaders we admire and support may conduct their personal lives in a manner we can't condone.

Conflicts between the viewpoints of people of different social groups can cause every manner of human strife from subtle discrimination to all-out war. Rather than trying to learn as much as we can about different cultures, to understand and get along with each other, we often regard the other with suspicion, fear, and defensiveness. This leads ultimately to anger, hate, and aggression, which harms us all.

Conflicts also arise between old beliefs and changing times. For example, cultural paradigms have had to undergo enormous changes as societies moved from agricultural to industrial to technological ages. Different values and focus are reflected in the metaphors of each age. Stories and images of nature and harvesting abound in agricultural societies, while the Western industrial age brought mechanical metaphors such as families and businesses being viewed and run as "well-oiled machines." Now we have a proliferation of computer, space travel, and high-tech weapons metaphors.

All of these conflicts—within ourselves, between us and others, between various social groups, and between old and new eras in time—signal a need for reexamining old beliefs, discarding those that no longer work for our highest well-being, and finding or creating new ones. Individually and collectively, our myths, parables, and metaphors evolve as we do.

Our Vantage Point

When I go to the theatre, I don't like to sit in the front row. I don't feel I can see as well from such a vantage point. I'm distracted by details, such as a piece of tape on the floor or a dancer's untied shoelace. Farther back, I gain a broader perspective of the entire stage. Examining our personal and cultural mythologies gives us that kind of broader perspective. We can step back and look at our lives without the distractions of the *details*—the effects and manifestations of our mythologies.

By becoming more aware of the myths, parables, and metaphors underlying our beliefs and behaviors, we can learn to understand ourselves better. We can learn to understand others better when we attempt to recognize and respect their mythology, which may be very different from ours. We can learn the difference between making stereotypical generalizations and discovering underlying universal truths about what it means to be human. We can begin making conscious choices about the mythologies that promote our growth and well-being, and that empower us to bridge the gaps of communication with others.

In this book, we'll examine our own myths, parables, and metaphors that affect every aspect of our lives and choices. We'll reflect on the stories of our lives and the meanings we give to them. We'll discover our freedom and responsibility in choosing our own mythology. We'll keep what's good for us, change what needs changing, and let go of what is no longer useful. We'll begin creating a mythology for ourselves that enhances our highest well-being and allows us to continue learning and evolving. We'll learn from both the old and the new.

We'll also examine the mythologies of our larger communities, such as religion, business, education, government, politics, and science. We'll explore the differences and similarities of various social mythologies, as well as common meanings and potentially unifying themes. We'll begin to see why communication can sometimes seem so difficult, and discover ways we can consciously make it better.

We're living in a time of extremely rapid change and

ever-increasing awareness of our global interconnected-ness. It is now more important than ever to better understand ourselves and others, to recognize and respect our diverse mythologies, while finding and creating universal ones. We now have the technology but not the language—the common mythology—we need to communicate with the whole world in positive ways.

It's time now for us to begin *consciously connecting*—with ourselves, each other, and the entire human community. It's time to discover and create our personal meanings, our collective meanings as social groups, and the meanings we can all share, worldwide. It's time—if I may use a metaphor—to start *building bridges*.

CHAPTER ONE

The Stories of Your Life

*Weaving your memories into a meaningful sequence of
stories about your past can deepen your relationship
with your own mythology, and place your
self-understanding in a richer context.*
—DAVID FEINSTEIN AND STANLEY KRIPPNER

According to legend, Saint Veronica was a woman of
Jerusalem who took off her veil and compassionately
wiped the blood and sweat from Jesus Christ's face
when he stumbled and fell while carrying his cross to
Calvary. She was an ordinary woman—not a martyred
saint who died some unspeakably gory death. She saw
something awful being done and, for a moment, forgot
herself to perform an act of kindness.

Growing up, I always thought that must have taken
tremendous courage—to push her way through the
crowd, to remove her veil in public, to defy the Roman
guards, to express herself through the simple act of
helping Jesus who was suffering. She couldn't stop
what was happening, but she did what she could. I
always admired that.

Veronica literally comes from the Latin word "veritas"
meaning truth. To me, her story is about being true to

yourself and your beliefs, regardless of what the rest of the crowd is saying or doing. It's about doing what you can, fearlessly, regardless of the things you can't do anything about. It's about having the courage of your convictions.

I don't know whether Saint Veronica really existed or whether she really did what the legend says she did. It doesn't matter. Her story is one of the stories of my life. I've used it to inform my worldview and guide my behavior. I've looked to it for inspiration when I felt I had to take a stand, or when I needed support for an unpopular viewpoint.

As mythologist Joseph Campbell pointed out, it's only when we insist on interpreting legends, myths, and fairy tales *literally* that we get into trouble and miss the point of them. Therefore, what's important here is not the literal truth of any of the stories of our lives, but the symbolic meaning we can derive from them and the help they can give us in understanding our world and making our choices.

The stories of our lives began at birth, and, when we look at our family histories, even before birth. As soon as we learned to understand language at all, stories became an important part of our lives. Basically, the stories of our lives fell into two categories: those we were told by others, and those we made up for ourselves based on our perceptions and personal experiences. Whether or not they were actually true or factual, all of these stories together made up the jigsaw puzzle of our complete worldview.

FAMILY STORIES

There were two kinds of stories we were told by others: stories of our family, and stories of fiction, fairy tales, fables, and other children's entertainment. Our family stories told us about who we were, who our ancestors were, what our family was like, and where we fit into that picture. They also told us about our family's place in larger communities, and consequently, our own.

We may have been told that our birth was either a "mistake" or a great event. We may have learned that our mother's pregnancy and labor were particularly difficult or wonderful and joyous. Our parents may have told us they would have preferred a child of the opposite gender. We may have heard stories about our parents' courtship, wedding, and life together before we were born. How our name was chosen, who our relatives were, and our family's religious and political affiliations were likely all explained to us through stories early in our lives. These, along with all the other family stories we were told—and some we secretly overheard or observed as curious children do—taught us a great deal about our identity and self-image.

Our Place in the Family

Zina says she's always felt that her birth ruined her parents' lives. "They were opera singers in Italy," she explains. "I was an 'accident.' At first, everyone thought I was so cute. They'd take turns taking care of me backstage while my parents worked. But as I got older and more mobile, it got harder and harder for my parents to travel with the company and take care of me when they were working, so they finally had to quit. They came back to the States and went into business."

Zina grew up on stories of her parents' days in the opera company. "It gave me a very rich storehouse of fantasies in one way, but in another way, it also made me feel guilty," she says. "They had really *loved* it; they had really been *happy*—before I was born. I've always felt responsible for taking that away from them."

Our families told us all kinds of things about ourselves. Our birth order may have labeled us the *responsible eldest* or the *spoiled baby* of the family. We may have learned to see ourselves as bright, dumb, creative, pretty, talented, or funny based on stories about ourselves when we were younger. Hearing, "You were always like that," may have created roles for us to live up to, or *down* to, in our minds.

We may often have heard stories about other relatives, particularly if we were named after one of them. Ed says that in his family, he's still known as "Little Ed," and his father as "Big Ed." He says, "When I was growing up, I always tried to be just like my dad. People in my family were always saying I got this trait or that talent from him. But then, when I was a teenager, I rebelled. I didn't want to be *just like* anybody. I wanted to be *me*. I guess I really went the other way, trying to be the opposite of my dad in everything."

Many of us outgrow this kind of adolescent rebellion to find that we are indeed like our parents or other relatives in some ways. But we often have to struggle against our family-assigned persona to find our true self, which also includes the ways in which we are different, and the ways in which we are continually growing and changing.

Our Family's Identity

A big part of our personal identity came from our family's identity. We heard stories that taught us, either directly or by implication, whether our parents, relatives, and ancestors were happy or unhappy, successful or unsuccessful, leaders or followers, victims or survivors. We may have concluded that we were, or should be, the same.

For example, the amount and kind of education our family members have received becomes a story for us to emulate. If we grew up hearing, "Everyone in our family goes to college," it affected us quite differently than growing up hearing, "You'll be the first of our family to be able to go to college." One implies a precedent to be lived up to as a member of the group, while the other expresses a special role or task to fulfill that will affect the entire family's identity.

On the other hand, we may have been discouraged from going to college if it was considered outside our family's identity. One woman says that in her family, college was referred to as a part of "the bourgeois establishment," and consequently, not something she felt comfortable pursuing, even though her high school grades were good. Other family stories may teach that "private schools are better than public schools," or that "private schools are only for rich brats." Whatever our family stories regarding education, they reflected specific attitudes and behaviors for us to follow.

The same kinds of stories were set up for us regarding the kinds of work done by our relatives and ancestors. We may feel pressured to follow in the footsteps of those who have gone before us, or to chart a new course for the benefit of the group. "My child, the doctor," for example, may be an ambition we wish to fulfill for our parents, to complete their story of struggle and sacrifice with a happy ending.

Our Family and the Rest of the World

Our upbringing was full of stories that illustrated our family's position in relation to the rest of the world. Our ethnicity, religion, political leanings, and socioeconomic status were reflected in and conveyed to us through these stories. Incidents in our family history may have become parables with morals such as:

Other people are prejudiced against us.
We're better than other people.
Other people are better than us.
We're different than other families.

Our families may have taught us these parables in an attempt to protect us from harm or hurt feelings. The parables may also have filled us with preset expectations and assumptions about ourselves, others, and the world.

Except for Native Americans, most people in the United States have ancestors who came here from someplace else. While Native Americans have their own family histories of displacement and change, many other Americans come from families who immigrated to the United States for a variety of reasons. Some

European immigrants came in the past century looking for a better life, more religious or political freedom, or greater economic opportunities. In more recent years, some people have come from Southeast Asia to escape wars and other problems in their homelands. Many Mexican refugees continue to seek relief from poverty by emigrating—illegally, if necessary—to the United States.

If our ancestors were immigrants, their reasons for coming and what they found here can make a tremendous difference in the way we perceive everything from our government to our next-door neighbors. If they came here to escape the Holocaust, your family stories will be very different than if you are African-American and your ancestors came here against their will or if you're Anglo-Saxon and your ancestors have prospered here since the days of colonization. The particular stories of our ancestors became myths and parables that guided our family's view of the rest of the world and our place in it. These parables teach us a great deal about who we should associate with, where we should live and work, what lifestyles our family approves of, and who we are in the world.

FICTION AND FAIRY TALES

We grew up with fiction from many sources—fables, fairy tales, myths, Bible stories, television, comics, and movies, to name a few. While all these stories contributed to our worldview, there are differences in the ways they did that. Some provided role models for us to emulate directly, while others set up fantasies which clearly could not be duplicated in the real world, but which taught specific values or beliefs through symbolic characters and events.

Essentially, a fable or parable is a clear moral edict with an example attached to it. Fairy tales are entertaining fantasies, always with a happy ending. This is very important to encourage children that problems can be resolved and difficulties overcome. Fairy tales offer hope.

Classical myths, such as ancient Greek and Roman stories of gods and goddesses, were once literally interpreted explanations of the universe. They are still told, but as symbolic representations of universal themes—human nature, the meaning of life, and how we should live. Like fairy tales, they often use metaphors, such as those personifying animals, trees, or the sun, moon, and stars. The Native American reference to "Mother Earth" is an example of symbolic representation of our relationship to the planet, which is not literally our mother, but brings forth and nourishes life in all its forms. Myths, whether a Greek odyssey or Native American vision quest, are usually stories of a particular hero and his or her experiences. The hero or heroine must overcome various obstacles and arrive at a destination, which usually is not a happy-ever-after solution, but more of a higher understanding of reality.

All of these fictions—fables, fairy tales, and myths—help us sort out our inner struggles, understand our outer world, and learn methods of acting effectively in life. They help facilitate our growth and encourage us to pursue it.

Our Own Special Stories

While we share many popular stories in our culture, no two people grow up with exactly the same fables, fairy tales, and other fictional stories. Even if we did, there would be differences in the ways they were presented to us, and our interpretations of them. Based on such factors as the availability of books, television programs, and storytellers, the particular people who read to us, and our own circumstances and most pressing issues, certain stories became especially important to us. We all have specific stories that stand out in our memories, whether we heard them from our parents, teachers, librarians, television, or we read them ourselves.

The dancers in the musical *A Chorus Line* spoke of seeing the movie *The Red Shoes* when they were growing up. The film was inspired by Hans Christian Andersen's moralistic fairy tale about the "sin" of pride. A young girl who loves her red shoes is enchanted to continue dancing in them until, finally, she must have her feet cut off and repent. In some versions, she actually dances to the point of utter exhaustion and dies. In the movie, a passionate young ballerina (who is dancing the Andersen fairy tale) must choose between her love for dancing and her love for a man—she chooses suicide. This tale, despite its clearly tragic ending, inspired many of these dancers to their profession. The passion to dance, whatever the cost, elevated their young minds above the drudgery and sacrifice of hours upon hours of practice.

Whether we grew up on Beatrix Potter, Bible stories, Grimm's Fairy Tales, or Winnie the Pooh, war stories, westerns, or science fiction, these stories helped us work through our particular issues and answered our questions about life. They helped to form our view of the world, our overriding paradigm, which in turn affected all our beliefs, attitudes, and actions—and still does.

Fantasies

Marge says she grew up on romantic fantasies she learned from the movies. "I think I got a lot of crazy ideas, watching all those old movies with heroines like Myrna Loy and Donna Reed," she says. "I really expected life to be like that—all white picket fences and happily-ever-after. When I grew up and found that it wasn't, I blamed myself, my husband, everything and everyone, instead of realizing that the picture I'd set up in my mind about how it would be was way off base."

While many women grew up with such romantic fantasies of love and marriage, many men grew up with images of strong, tough heroes. From westerns and war movies to superhero comics, men may have been fed a steady stream of messages about such topics as heroism, violence, and the treatment of women. Heroes like John Wayne and the fictional James Bond gave very different role models for growing boys than the women Marge described above.

These gender-role models may have set us up for confusion and difficulties in our adult life. As Marge said, we often blame everything and everyone for these difficulties, except the real culprit—our old unrealistic beliefs and fantasies. Fairy tales and other stories sometimes also promote useless guilt, fear, anxiety, and distorted images of people, relationships, and life. For example, a young girl's joy in red shoes and dancing is hardly cause for drastic punishment and recrimination. Many of us may have suffered such squelching of our youthful joys and now struggle through adulthood to recapture them.

Realistic Role Models

While young children need stories with happy endings in order to develop hope, older children and young adults also need realistic role models. Images of others achieving personal growth and learning through overcoming difficulties can provide a vicarious experience of growth in the reader's own mind.

It's important to remember that the stories we each grew up with impacted our image of ourselves, other people, and the world. They helped make our individual viewpoint exactly what it is. They may have been helpful sometimes, but also damaging in some ways to our self-image, relationships, or behavior. We're not examining them to blame someone for our problems, but to better understand how we came to view the world as we do. Then we can move on to improving that view for our own well-being and effective living.

THE STORYTELLER IN OURSELVES

The other stories of our lives are the ones we make up ourselves. Even the people closest to us—brothers and sisters, parents, friends, lovers or spouses—can never see through our eyes. We each experience and perceive the world in our own unique way, drawing our own conclusions. The specific incidents of our lives provide us with the stories that shape our view of reality, ourselves, and others. They give meaning to our past experiences and teach us lessons we can use in the future. We continue creating these stories for ourselves throughout our entire lives.

We can think of all the stories we've accumulated in our conscious and unconscious minds as a collection in a scrapbook or photo album. Each page or picture represents a moment in our life, a memory that has become a part of our history and, consequently, our present outlook. They're all symbols for parts of ourselves, our relationships, our world.

As we age, we can look back over the many stories of our lives and begin viewing them as an overall pattern, or progression, from incident A to period B to decision C, and so on. But such a perspective takes time to see, and we first need to look at each story to find its meaning and learn its lessons.

Early Stories

Each of us has a mental storehouse of stories from our early life, our childhood. These stories provided us with morals, or lessons, about how life is and how we should be. They revolve around the most important people and places in our young lives—family, school, church, and peer groups. They stand out in our memories because of something we learned from them. Often, they're so memorable because they showed us a truth or a side of life for the first time, or conflicted with something we already believed to be true.

Jim tells us about his first day of school. "The kindergarten teacher passed out these pieces of paper," he says. "Across the top the teacher had printed our name, and we were supposed to copy it over and over again. She said it was very important, so we could write our names on our artwork and other papers.

"I looked at my name written across the top of my sheet of paper," Jim remembers. "It was misspelled. I didn't think about how I knew it, or that I wasn't supposed to know it yet. I guess my parents must have taught me, but I didn't think about that—it was just something I *knew*. I told the teacher she'd misspelled my name, and she responded, 'How would you know?' She yelled at me to stop being difficult and causing trouble, and to start writing my name, like the other children, the way she'd spelled it. I insisted that it was spelled wrong and she told me I *had no business* telling her that, that I couldn't possibly know what I was talking about.

"I don't remember which way I wrote my name down on the page that day, but that first experience in school showed me that so-called experts and people in positions of authority aren't always right and don't necessarily know more than I do. It also taught me that school is not the only place you can learn things."

Childhood is filled with firsts, and these experiences become stories in our inner repertoire from which we draw information thereafter. If our first experiences with school, camp, church, sports, or social activities were unpleasant, those stories can become parables making us wary of subsequent experiences in those areas. On the other hand, positive firsts can set us up for positive future experiences.

Stories of Adolescence

Our teenage years are often the source of stories that involve inner turmoil and outer conflict. The space between childhood and adulthood is a time of rapid change. Letting go of some of the old comforts of the past and experimenting with new feelings, relationships, abilities, and experiences can be confusing and difficult. The physical and hormonal changes we experience can also make us particularly sensitive to all the other changes happening in our lives. There are many *firsts* and many *lasts* in adolescence. There are many lessons to learn about ourselves, others, and our world, which can affect us for many years into adulthood.

Carla tells us a parable from her sixteenth year. "I always loved reading and writing," she says. "When I was in high school, one of my teachers said that my writing was good and showed a lot of promise. She said I should write for the school paper and encouraged me to start keeping a journal. One day, I made the mistake of bringing my journal to school so I could write during my free hour. Some kids took it when I wasn't looking and read it. All my personal thoughts and feelings were broadcast all over the school. I was mortified. My best friend got it back for me and said, 'Never put anything in writing that you don't want to come back and haunt you.' I quit the school paper, went home and burned the journal, and didn't write another word until I was thirty."

Today, at forty, Carla is a successful journalist and published author. Not all the parables we learned over the years came with healthy, useful, or constructive morals. They taught us something at the time which may have protected us, helped us to survive or cope with a difficult situation or relationship, or served us in some other way. But when we recognize a negative effect in our adult lives, we can let go, as Carla eventually did, of any old morals that may be holding us back from a fuller, happier life.

Turning Points in Adulthood

As adults, we accumulate stories of our successes and failures, difficulties faced and overcome, and incidents that changed us and our lives in some way. Marriage or divorce, the birth of a child or the death of a loved one, illness, or recovery from an addiction can all be major turning points in our adult lives. These, along with countless other experiences, constitute our collection of stories from our adult years. These stories represent stages of our growth, lessons about ourselves and life. Sometimes they change our attitude or outlook a bit; other times they can change the course of our entire life.

A Realization

When Joe nearly died during his withdrawal from alcohol, he says he had been "waiting to die for a long time." But coming as close to death as Joe did awakened him to the realization that he didn't truly want to die.

"I thought I had resigned myself to dying," he says. "I knew I was drinking myself to death. I'd wake up in the morning with no feeling in my extremities—I had trouble picking things up with my fingers. I didn't like the way it felt, so I decided to quit drinking, and then I went into a real bad withdrawal." In the intensive care unit, Joe's vital signs stopped at one point, and his life was saved by a very alert nurse.

"I'd thought that I wanted to die," he says. "But when I was there, and it was so real, I knew it wasn't what I wanted. There I was dying, and it wasn't any better than living. It wasn't romantic, it wasn't dramatic, there was no poetry or light at the end of a long tunnel, or any of that wonderful stuff. I was just dying. That was it. And I realized that my impact on the world was just not going to be anymore. Life would just go on without me and I would quietly turn to dust. I knew then and there that I didn't want to die."

Joe's realization was a major turning point in his adult life. The experience became a powerful story he'll never forget. Joe says, "I feel like it was all about *time*—I'd wasted so much time. Now I feel like I have this big responsibility to use whatever time I have left really well." Our stories aren't always this dramatic or clear in their message. But if we make the effort to uncover and examine the stories of our lives, they can teach us valuable lessons about ourselves, others, and the world.

Relationship Stories

Each of our relationships has a history of stories connected with it. While our viewpoint and memories of these stories may differ from the other person's, our own perceptions create our view of ourselves, the other person, and the relationship. The collection of stories in our mind related to a particular relationship affects the way we feel about and behave in the relationship now.

Particularly in long-term relationships, such as

between spouses, parents and children, siblings, in-laws, and friends, we accumulate a long list of stories. They reflect times we felt close, times we felt hurt, times we experienced something special together, and times we overcame something difficult together. Some of them are wonderful, warm, treasured memories, while others are painful experiences we may wish we could forget. All of them contribute to the current problems and successes of our relationships.

Mary says that when she'd been married for twelve years, she and her husband had finally reached a point where they'd worked out a lot of problems and felt happy together. But, Mary says, old painful memories still haunted her. "I knew certain things would never happen again, that we'd both grown and changed a lot, and I was happy to be married to him," she explains. "But there were still all those old memories I couldn't get rid of. It was like I had all these old memories of when things were bad, but fewer recent memories of when things were good, and the old was contaminating the new."

Mary and her husband decided to separate briefly to make a clean break between the old and the new parts of their relationship. "We agreed on all the rules for the separation, so nothing could go wrong," she says. "Then we married each other again, even though we'd never actually gotten divorced. We just made up a little ceremony of our own and exchanged new vows. Now I have this clear delineation in my mind between our *first* marriage and our *current* marriage."

Mary and her husband created a story for themselves to mark a turning point in their relationship. Now their shared history includes a very clear-cut beginning of their new life together. This is one example of how we can always create new stories for ourselves whenever we need them.

TELLING OUR STORIES TO OURSELVES

Our memories are the stories we tell ourselves about our past experiences. We keep these stories in our minds, consciously and unconsciously, where they continue to affect our beliefs, attitudes, and actions. By pulling them out, dusting them off, and examining them carefully, we can learn to understand them, and ourselves, better. We can ask ourselves, *Where have I been? What did it mean? Where am I now? Where do I want to go?* and, *How can I get there?*

Journaling is one good way to examine the stories we keep in our mind. We can write out our memories and what we think they mean to us. Just the act of writing them often makes them become clearer to us somehow, or it changes the way we look at them. As we mature, our perspective changes, and it's sometimes very helpful to look at an old experience through new eyes. In his book *The Story of Your Life,* Dan Wakefield describes how "remembering and writing down our past from a spiritual perspective (that is, taking into account its meaning in the context of our life's journey) . . . we can sometimes see and understand it in a way that makes it different."

No one can completely erase at will certain memories from his or her consciousness and remain healthy and happy. But we can, as Wakefield suggests, "tame" our past memories by examining them from a new, more mature, perspective. Writing them out can help release them from the prison of our thoughts and, often, free us of old emotions that we'd attached to them. Distanced by time from old experiences, we can often look back to discover lessons we couldn't see when they occurred. This way, we can continue growing and learning all of our lives.

A Method to Release Our Stories

Journaling is a way to release these old stories without fear of other people's judgments and interference. A journal or diary is a special, *private* place for us to express ourselves and to work through any old stories we want. It is absolutely *ours,* and no one has the right to read it, unless we choose to share it with someone. We have seen from Carla's story that disrespecting this personal boundary can harm the trust in our relationships and our ability to express ourselves. So, hide it if you have to, but keep your journal as a special gift to yourself.

There are many simple writing exercises we can use to start examining the stories of our lives. We can choose a specific time in our life to write about, a particular relationship, or a special place. We can use metaphors to represent our outer circumstances or problems, or our inner feelings and beliefs. We can forget everything we were ever taught about the rules of grammar, spelling, and poetry, and write in any way that expresses what we think, feel, and remember.

One woman used a very simple metaphor to write the
following poem in her journal about her life in recovery:

i'm walking
without crutches now
it isn't easy
and it hurts
and sometimes
i fall down
but i'm walking
without crutches

i'm walking
without crutches
without chemicals
or fantasies
of romance
or delusions
of grandeur
or a crowd
of cheering fans

a little money
i admit
goes a long way
but not that far
poverty
in fact
can be a crutch
an excuse
lack
can keep you busy
occupied
trying to get
obtain
acquire
chasing after
or blaming

whatever
you don't have

i'm walking
without crutches now
slowly
taking one step at a time
all the while
wondering
where i'm going
and why

Whether we use poetry, story-writing, or any other exercise, our goal is always self-understanding. We're not trying to *impress* anyone with our literary skill or creativity, we're trying to *express* some of what's inside us out into our consciousness and the world—like expressing juice from an orange. Other writing exercises to help us clarify the stories of our lives appear on the next page. There is also a list of helpful books on journaling in the bibliography at the end of this book.

TELLING OUR STORIES TO OTHERS

You might want to read some of your journal stories and exercises to others who you trust and who understand the goal of self-discovery. Self-disclosure to others can be helpful in many ways. This method of examining our stories is used in Twelve Step meetings, as well as traditional forms of therapy with a counselor, psychiatrist, psychologist, or clergyperson.

Trust is vitally important in this method of storytelling, and we must respect ourselves enough to choose our audiences carefully. We don't go around spilling our guts to anyone who will listen. We share ourselves on a deep spiritual level with another human being. Putting our stories out there for another person to hear and comment on can make us feel vulnerable, but if we choose a trustworthy person who cares about us and respects us, we can learn a great deal from his or her perspective and also from just speaking our stories aloud.

USING OUR STORIES

We can use all of the stories of our lives, from our family stories to our favorite fairy tales to the memory-stories in our minds, to help us understand ourselves better. We can pull them into clear view and see the effects they've had on our self-image and our view of other people and the world. We can stop being afraid of the ones we don't like to think about and release the power we've given them. We can take charge of our mental scrapbooks and all the stories we've collected in there. We can treasure the lovely helpful ones, and let go of the old self-defeating ones. We can use them all for our own higher consciousness and true well-being. That's what they're there for.

EXERCISES

Family Stories:
   Think about, write about, or tell someone about the family stories . . .

   that told you your family's identity.
   that told you your place or role in the family.
   that revealed family secrets.

about your parents (background, marriage, work, hobbies, etc.).

about each specific family member.

about your ancestors.

Complete the following sentences about your family:

"We always . . ."
"We never . . ."
"We're good at . . ."
"We love . . ."
"We hate . . ."

Fictional Stories:

Which myths, fairy tales, fables, comics, and other children's stories do you remember? Which were your favorites? Which characters did you identify with most? How did you relate the stories to reality? What did they teach you? Can you see their effects in your outlook and behavior even now?

Choose a mythological or fairy tale character that represents you, and rewrite the story to give it the best ending for your true well-being. What can you learn from this? What can you use in your real life?

Personal Stories:

Write or tell a story about an incident from your life and give it a one-sentence moral. (The moral need not be true or good for you—this exercise is for self-discovery, and we sometimes discover that we hold self-defeating beliefs.)

Write or tell one story each about a specific incident

in your childhood, your adolescence, and your adulthood. Choose moments in your life that you would call
turning points, milestones, or transformations, and write
a story about each.

Look at an old photograph of yourself, and write a
story about the person you were then.

Finish the following sentences by writing a story:

The first time I ever . . .
The best time of my life . . .
The scariest time of my life . . .
My favorite place in the world . . .

CHAPTER TWO

Personal Evolution

*In the later years of a lifetime, looking back over
the course of one's days . . . one may find it difficult
to resist the notion of the course of one's biography
as comparable to that of a cleverly constructed novel.*
—JOSEPH CAMPBELL

When we ask people to tell us the stories of their
lives, they usually respond by telling us where they
were born, where they've lived, and what kind of work
they've done. Sometimes they talk about their family of
origin or their marriages and children. But if we ask
them to tell us about the most important events and
experiences of their lives, their *turning points,* a different story emerges. People tell of coping with divorces,
deaths of loved ones, and serious illnesses. They
describe automobile accidents, financial ruin, periods of
depression, and addictions left behind. They tell stories
of survival, learning, and growth. They talk about who
they have been and who they have become.

These are the stories of our heroic journeys through
the evolutionary process of our lives. We are each the
hero of our own epic drama. The most significant
events in our lives represent chapters in this unfolding

story. We can look back over these events and begin seeing the shape, pattern, and character of our life story.

ARCHETYPES

Psychologist Carl G. Jung coined the phrase "collective unconscious" to describe the underlying common experience of being human. He wrote that "personal unconscious rests on a deeper layer, which does not derive from personal experience and is not a personal acquisition but is inborn. . . . This part of the unconscious is not individual but universal." Jung identified the contents of the collective unconscious as "instinctual" roles and situations common throughout humanity, which he labeled the *archetypes.*

The most common way of looking at Jung's theory of the archetypes is through roles or figures that reflect universal aspects of being human. Hero, mother, child, martyr, warrior, and lover are but a few common archetypal figures. Each is a viewpoint, a way of making meaning and finding purpose in specific times and situations of life. In various circumstances, we fill the role of dependent child, nurturing mother, or martyr, sacrificing for a higher purpose. Occasionally, we must take a stand as the warrior, but we are always the hero of our own life story.

The Hero's Journey

One of the oldest known stories is Homer's *The Odyssey,* a tale of one man's journey through a series of trials and tribulations. Odysseus, in his ten years of wandering on his way home from the Trojan War, becomes the hero of his own life by experiencing and overcoming all manner of obstacles, temptations, and setbacks. The *Hero* archetype reflects our journey through life, facing and dealing with all the "dragons" in our way, both inside and outside of us.

Each one of us has the life story of a hero, even if our life doesn't seem particularly heroic. For some of us, our *dragons* have been opposition from others, physical impairments, or unhappy childhood experiences. For others, they may have been addictions, illnesses, earthquakes, financial disasters, or sudden widowhood. We all have many dragons to confront in a lifetime—both within our own psyches and our outer lives. The specific forms our own dragons have taken create our life story, or *hero's journey.*

"I don't exactly think of myself as a hero," says Faye, a middle-aged African-American woman who has achieved executive status in her career. "I never jumped in the lake to save anyone's life," she laughs. "But I guess I've had to slay a few dragons along the way. Sometimes the dragon was my own self-doubt or a tough teacher in school. Other times it was people saying I *couldn't* do this or I *shouldn't* do that. In my career, I figured if no one was going to give me a chance, I'd make my own chances. This is *my* life, *my* journey, and I have to face *myself* in the end. Now I'm able to help some of these young folks coming up, but I know they too have to slay their own dragons. That's the way you find out who you are and what you can do."

Faye didn't become the hero of her own life by performing some publicly acclaimed act of bravery, but by many smaller life- and self-affirming acts. Being the heroes of our own lives doesn't mean making one grand gesture, ensuring our salvation forever. We continue confronting and slaying dragons all our lives.

Hitting Bottom

At some time or other, all heroes venture into the *underworld*—the depths of fear, rage, or despair. It is always necessary in a hero's tale to take this mythological trip before transformation to new heights of maturity, understanding, success, and happiness are possible. In his book *A Guide for the Perplexed,* E. F. Schumacher explains, "Only if we *know* that we have actually descended into *infernal regions* . . . can we summon the courage and imagination needed for a 'turning around,' a *metanoia.* This then leads to seeing the world in a new light."

This new light is shed upon the world for us only after we have faced the darkness, the *shadow* of our human experience. When we stop avoiding and denying this part of ourselves, we discover that it consists of nothing more than ordinary human fears, doubts, and sorrow. Even a blustering monster of anger within us can be unmasked as the defensive reaction of a hurt child. As the hero of our own life, we confront these inner dragons and either slay them or make peace with them. This is a turning point that opens us up to new possibilities we couldn't see before.

The hero's journey represents a series of such turning points—of dragons we've confronted and trips we've taken into our dark side or shadow. Examining our lives in this way shows us how our personal mythology has grown along with us. It changes as we do, evolving and maturing to serve us better in the future. Such maturity grows from our conscious experiences along the path of our hero's journey.

GROWING THROUGH THE CHAKRAS

According to ancient Hindu and Buddhist teachings, human beings contain seven levels of energy called the *chakras*. The *chakras* are centered in seven areas of the body, from the base of the spine to the crown of the head. A corresponding spectrum of colors is associated with the *chakras,* from red on the lower end to purple at the top. Survival energy, associated with life, is centered at the base of the spine; sexual energy in the abdomen; the energy of power at the solar plexus or stomach area; compassion at the heart; communication at the throat; knowledge at the forehead or "third eye"; and enlightenment at the crown of the head.

We can trace our personal development through the levels of energy the chakras represent. In the first, or lowest, chakra, we develop our abilities for survival. In infancy and childhood, we become physically mobile, learn to recognize hunger and other basic needs, and develop means of getting those needs met. We learn to feed ourselves and take care of our bodies in basic ways.

In the next level, we discover the sexual aspect of ourselves. In adolescence, our bodies and emotions conspire to provide our sexual awakening. This doesn't mean that we are mature enough to make the best decisions for ourselves in this area, nor capable of healthy, mature sexual relationships, but simply that sexuality becomes an undeniable part of our self and our self-image.

The third chakra represents *power,* often manifesting in money and success. We discover ourselves as an effective person in the world—we can make choices, create changes, achieve goals. We learn about our power *to* make things happen, and also our power *over* others.

Up to this point, it's easy to follow the growth of a human being into adulthood. But now the chakras begin to symbolize higher energies: compassion, communication, knowledge, and spiritual enlightenment. While most of us may believe we possess and express these higher energies at least some of the time, it seems this is where most of us get stuck.

Compassion

The fourth chakra is a turning point. Whereas the first three chakras focus on ourselves, the fourth turns outward, to recognition of our interconnectedness with all other beings. All the higher chakras are extensions of this new perspective of ourselves as part of one whole life in the universe. The word we use for this life-changing recognition, this discovery of our true place in the universe, is "compassion."

We hold up models of true compassion—people such as Mother Teresa or the Dalai Lama—as examples to emulate. But mostly, we don't think it's even possible for many of us to come close to such devoted service to other human beings. We don't think of ourselves as part of each other, of one whole human family. We can hardly empathize with our own loved ones, much less total strangers all across the world. It seems more automatic for us to always choose sides rather than extend our understanding and compassion to *all*. True compassion is still an *ideal* rather than a reality for most of us.

Sometimes we may even fear appearing foolish for expressing compassion. The level of true compassion finds harmony between seeing the world and everything in it as it really is, understanding our interrelatedness to it all, and refusing to contribute to the harm. Most of us, however, are stuck well below that level of compassion, feeling either insensitive to the pain of others or overwhelmed by it.

The level of true compassion requires a mature understanding of our interconnectedness with all other people and life forms, as well as the concept of healthy detachment. Sometimes the most loving, helpful thing to do is let go; other times our indifference to the pain around us contributes to it and causes our own pain. True compassion is a healthy balance between feeling for others, doing what we can to help, and letting go of what we can't change.

Our Search for Meaning: The Higher Chakras

The higher chakras represent our search for *meaning*, the development of our deep understanding of all we see, feel, think, and do. The highest issues we can attempt to resolve are represented by the fifth, sixth, and seventh chakras.

The fifth chakra represents the energy of communication, of true communion with other human beings. E. F. Schumacher calls this true communication a "meeting of minds," and writes that it requires both self-knowledge and empathy for others—the precise qualities of the first four chakras. But much of what passes for communication in our world is really manipulation, deceit, confusion, and impression. We seem to use it more to keep ourselves apart, to protect ourselves from one another, than to consciously connect.

The sixth chakra, located in the forehead or "third eye," represents knowledge. True knowledge goes beyond mere facts to include insight and understanding, which give the facts their *meaning*. But a great deal of what we call *knowledge* is really opinion, assumption, hearsay, or superstition. It's difficult for most of us to sort through all this and separate the wheat from the chaff—or the knowledge from the nonsense. And without the perspective of true compassion and the ability of true communication with others, our knowledge is all but useless. It can even be dangerous.

Seeking Spiritual Enlightenment

As for spiritual enlightenment, the seventh chakra, only a handful of people in the history of the world can claim to have reached the mystical understanding of a Lao-Tzu, the Buddha, Mohammed, Moses, or Jesus Christ. Most of us struggle with interpreting the teachings of such spiritual leaders. Many of us never even have the opportunity of being exposed to their ideas. Spiritual growth takes time and effort, and many of us consider it a luxury reserved for people who have cut themselves off from daily work, family, and their social lives. Often, we don't even bother to seek spiritual enlightenment, or we seek it where it will never be found—outside ourselves.

Climbing the Chakra Ladder

So it seems, in light of the chakra model, that most of us spend our lives recycling issues of survival, sex, and power—the lowest three chakras. But if we were to concentrate on resolving these issues and becoming more truly compassionate, we might make a giant step toward real maturity. We can use the chakra model to help us to organize our efforts and create positive goals toward our next steps of personal evolution.

If we recognize where we are on the chakra ladder, we can focus on reinforcing the steps we have already taken and work on the steps ahead. We can let go of issues we've outgrown, and move on to more mature themes—higher chakras. We can see our personal evolution from the perspective of the chakra metaphor and use this view to clarify where we've been, where we are, and where we need to go.

AGES AND STAGES OF LIFE

In the 1950s, psychologist Erik H. Erikson identified eight stages of psychological development. Erikson's stages still stand as the most commonly accepted model of psychological development though a lifetime.

Erikson labeled the stages as follows: Infancy, Early Childhood, Play Age, School Age, Adolescence, Young Adulthood, Adulthood, and Old Age. Each stage has a particular corresponding issue to be faced and resolved. Respectively, these are trust, autonomy, initiative, industry, identity, intimacy, generativity, and integrity.

By the time we reach puberty, in Erikson's model, we have already passed through four of the eight stages. The remaining stages—Adolescence, Young Adulthood, Adulthood, and Old Age—each carry particular developmental tasks, crises, or lessons to be worked through. Problems arise due to unfinished tasks, unresolved crises, or negative lessons learned in our previous stages.

It can take our entire lives to resolve and balance all the "critical psychological conflicts" of personal evolution. We can use Erikson's model to think about the stories from various stages in our lives. We can learn about all the aspects of our psyche, develop them in the most positive ways for us, and integrate them into our whole selves.

OUR HIERARCHY OF NEEDS

Psychologist Abraham Maslow developed another model we can use to help clarify our development through various experiences and stages of life. Maslow ranked five levels of human needs in order of their importance. Basic survival or physiological needs come first, then safety or security needs, love or belonging needs, esteem needs, and finally, the need for self-actualization.

Physiological needs are basic physical needs including air, food, water, sleep, activity, and stimulation.

Our need for safety and security means protection from such threats as wild animals, violent weather, assault, murder, and other immediate emergencies. This also includes our various "insurance" plans for saving or investing money; job security; and financial coverage for unexpected medical expenses. We all need to feel safe from possible disasters.

Belongingness, or love needs, are reflected in our desire for relationships. We form groups, make friends, and join cliques, clubs, gangs, cults, and various other communities to satisfy this need. From our intimate relationships to casual friendships, working associations, families and neighbors, we fill our lives with relationships. We form bonds with other human beings to avoid feeling rejected, lonely, and rootless.

Our "esteem needs" include the need for self-confidence and also recognition from others of our competence and effectiveness. We need to feel capable and confident and to have others see us that way too. As many people have learned, these needs are *not* satisfied through achieving fame or an inflated public image, but rather through true respect from others for our abilities and accomplishments.

Self-actualization is the term Maslow used to describe our highest level of development. When all other needs are satisfactorily met, we need to become and express our highest, truest, best selves.

Meeting Our Needs

Maslow's model is simple to understand if we look at a few examples. While all of the needs are present in each of us, they must be met in a certain order: If we have no access to food or water, our need for love or self-expression doesn't seem very important. If our physical safety is in jeopardy, it doesn't matter much whether or not we feel accepted by our peer group.

When our body is in pain, we don't care much about being recognized by others for our achievements. In other words, *first things first*.

Once a need is met, we can recognize it and move on, evolving up the hierarchy of needs. But sometimes we get mentally or emotionally stuck in one or more of the lower level needs, even though the needs are being satisfied. We may cling to fears of losing what we have, even when there is no real basis for these fears. For example, we may feel we can never acquire enough money to feel secure. Or we may never feel safe or loved enough, no matter how safe or loved we really are. Facing and resolving such fears allow us to grow and evolve to higher levels, and ultimately to self-actualization.

A Universal Need

If we view development to self-actualization as a universal need, we can begin understanding others whose lower needs are not being met, rather than judging them for not reaching higher levels of development. We can stop feeling guilty or self-indulgent for wanting to develop ourselves to our highest potential. We can use this model to help us understand and gently encourage ourselves and others to fulfill all of our needs.

When we work at getting our needs met, we have to learn where we can and cannot expect to find fulfillment. We have to take responsibility for meeting our own legitimate needs and let go of looking for rescuers. We have to allow ourselves to develop through the hierarchy of needs, mindful of continually satisfying them all.

Looking Back

We human beings are symbolic, interpretive crea-
tures. We want to know what everything *means*. We
look back over our lives and try to find the meaning in
events, experiences, and relationships. While people
seem naturally to review their life in later years, to discover its shape and meaning, we can do this at any
time. We can begin looking back over the stories that
make up our life's total picture right now, whatever our
age. The overall story of our life is *ours,* to write any
way we choose. But we must become conscious of our
personal evolution to this point in order to choose what
it all means and where it might go from here.

We can use any of the metaphors, theories, or structures we've discussed in this chapter to clarify our own
personal evolution, to discover our own life story, and
to find our own *meanings*. As we trace our development through our hero's journey, the chakra ladder,
Erikson's stages of life, or Maslow's hierarchy of needs,
we can begin to see how our life has flowed from one
event, lesson, or issue into another. We can begin to
notice a motif, or character, to it all. We can see how
we've found opportunities to learn what we needed to
learn and to fulfill our particular potentialities. We can
see how the stories of our life have blended into one
story, our own life story, our life's *meaning*.

EXERCISES

Our Life in Decades

Think back over your life in decades: your childhood, teens, twenties, thirties, forties, fifties, and so on.

For each decade, think about the following questions: What were your priorities? Your beliefs in God/religion/spirituality? Your politics, passions, problems, and needs? How has your worldview changed over time?

The Dragons We Have Overcome

Write or tell someone your life story, casting yourself as the hero. What "dragons" have you overcome, worked through, resolved, or resisted? Draw pictures of all the people and places that were important to you along the way.

The Chakra Ladder

Visualize your life in terms of the *chakra* ladder. Think through the issues of the first three chakras (survival, sex, and power) in relation to your life; determine areas of unresolved problems; plan specific ways to resolve them and work toward greater compassion, communication, knowledge, and spiritual enlightenment.

The Eight Stages

Use *Erikson's eight stages of life* to look back over your life and identify the stages you have lived through and their corresponding issues. Do you see any unresolved issues from earlier stages? How are they affecting you now? How can you resolve them? Where can you go from there?

Maslow's Method

Use *Maslow's hierarchy of needs* to determine which needs are priorities for you right now. How do you identify them in your particular life circumstances? How can you get them met? How do you define self-actualization? How can you work toward reaching it?

CHAPTER THREE

Conflicting Mythologies

*A world view is so fundamental that we realize we have
one only when confronted by an alternative.*
—ROBERT AUGROS AND GEORGE STANCIU

Our personal mythology is so much a part of our
thinking that we can't really be aware of it and its
effects on us until we step outside it. We take our
worldview or belief systems for granted until something
happens to make us look at them in a new way.

Basically, two kinds of things can shake up our
worldview or mythology: things that happen *outside* us
and things that happen *inside* us. No one else's worldview is exactly the same as ours and our own cannot
be the same as it's been at any point in the past—it
changes, grows, and evolves as we do. These differences—both within ourselves and between ourselves
and others—can create conflicts for us.

CONFLICTS WITH OTHER PEOPLE

There are many times and ways in which our mythology collides with other people's. When we encounter
someone whose experiences and background are different than ours; when we consciously choose an

opposing viewpoint on a specific problem or issue; or when someone with whom we're trying to relate is at a different stage of his or her development than we are, difficulties can arise in the relationships.

Our responses to these conflicts vary, depending on the nature of our relationship, our level of tolerance for differences, and our openness to diversity and growth. A tolerance for differences means we don't feel threatened by different viewpoints; we can accept that other people won't always agree with us. Being open to diversity means being able to learn from other mythologies and to allow our perspective to grow.

Different relationships can create different responses to conflict. For example, in a working relationship, we may be able to ignore differences in viewpoint as long as they don't interfere with our work. But in our personal relationships, we may care more about truly understanding others and having them understand us. In the beginning of a relationship, we may let differences pass or even be unable to see them. Later, when we know each other better, those differences may cause greater conflict or even become intolerable.

Reacting to Conflicts

Sometimes the differences between us and others just aren't important—we can simply agree to disagree. Other times we have to take a stand, such as when we're being harmed in a relationship or feel our values or ethics are being violated. But sometimes our defensiveness is triggered when we are faced with a different worldview, and we react with anger. We may verbally attack the other person, deriding their credibility, motives, or honesty.

We can always remember to calm down and take a moment to ask ourselves *why* we feel so threatened by another's point of view. Are we really unsure of our own? Are we afraid people won't like or accept us if we don't agree with them all the time? Are we listening to what the other person is trying to say or just reacting to feeling attacked in some way?

We can think about Maslow's hierarchy of needs and ask ourselves what needs we fear losing or being deprived of by another's viewpoint. By examining ourselves this way, we can avoid filling our personal mythology with defensive views. We can consciously choose our worldview or personal mythology rather than letting it become nothing more than a reactionary defense against imagined threats from others.

If we are open-minded, exposure to a different viewpoint or mythology can sometimes reinforce our own. Other conflicts can cause us to grow, opening up to new ways of looking at things. Conflicts can either stretch and change our perspective or deepen and enrich our old beliefs. Either way, we have to open our eyes to see the other viewpoint before we can choose our response to it.

Self-Knowledge Comes First

Everything we have explored in this book thus far has been to uncover and understand our own personal worldview, or mythology. This self-understanding is necessary before we can understand others and our conflicts with them. By examining and learning to understand ourselves, we can broaden our perspective on other people's thoughts and intentions.

Clear, open, honest, and productive communication with others is possible only when we start with a basis of self-knowledge. As we attempt to translate other people's symbols—their words and actions—we can use a greater storehouse of understanding to interpret their meanings. We can also know when to say "I don't understand; please explain" rather than jumping to conclusions and making assumptions.

When we have done the inner work necessary for true self-knowledge, we develop capacities for compassion and unselfishness. These qualities grow from our loss of fear and defensiveness as we learn who we truly are. We can stop living and conducting our relationships only on the shallowest surface and begin opening up to true communication and understanding. This means developing *empathy* toward others.

Empathy

We can never really look at the world through any eyes other than our own. But the clearer our own vision—the greater our self-knowledge and understanding—the easier it is to imagine what others might see or feel or think.

Sometimes just admitting that we really don't know how things look from another's viewpoint can help us open up to greater understanding of our differences with others. Once we have acquired self-knowledge, we can begin trying to see through other people's eyes and feel what others feel. Empathizing with others doesn't necessarily mean we'll end up agreeing with them, but we'll better understand them and be better able to respect their viewpoint, however it may differ from our own.

Empathy means rising above the insistence on winners and losers, on who is right and who is wrong. It means understanding and accepting that there are different ways of looking at everything. It means spending our time and energy trying to understand our own and the other person's view and underlying mythology, rather than defending ourselves against the threat to our ego of having someone disagree with us.

Exercises in role-reversal, or trading places, with someone whose mythology conflicts with ours can help us let go of our fears and begin to develop some empathy in our relationships. There's an old children's story about a man who stays home to do his wife's chores while she goes into town to do his work—they had each assumed the other's job to be easier. At the end of the day, each of them has a much better understanding of the other's viewpoint, and they return to their usual roles with new respect and empathy in their relationship.

This story metaphorically illustrates how we can learn to understand each other better by opening up to switching viewpoints—looking at things from different perspectives. Stretching ourselves to see through another's viewpoint doesn't mean we have to give up our own. It means our own viewpoint gets larger and more inclusive. It means more knowledge and understanding for us, which gives us a more informed and healthier worldview.

Win-Win Resolutions

A common response to conflict is to always find someone *right* and someone else *wrong*. In this view, there can be only winners and losers in any conflict, and everyone's personal mythology is either ignored or judged. The only possible outcome is for one party to be persuaded to agree with or to unwillingly surrender to the other. This way of viewing conflict is based on fear, anger, and lack of self-knowledge.

One way of responding from this viewpoint is the defensive position that *I'm always right*. From this perspective, differing viewpoints are always treated with hostility. Another side of the same viewpoint is to decide that *I'm always wrong*. We may believe that whenever someone disagrees with us, they must be right and we must be wrong. These two attitudes are opposite sides of the same win-lose view of conflict.

But there is another way we can look at conflicts between people's mythologies. We can replace our win-lose viewpoint with a win-win perspective. We both win when we grow in understanding of ourselves and each other, when our mythology stretches to include new information, and when no one is harmed or a viewpoint ignored.

Our real, true universal needs are for *all* of us to live, grow, and prosper. We all benefit from each other's love, health, peace, joy, and success. Recognizing our differences honestly and learning to share, grow, compromise, and help each other can bring us together. Our diverse mythologies can expand and enrich human life everywhere if we learn to truly see them, respect them, and use them for our mutual benefit.

THE PEACEFUL WARRIOR

Sometimes a conflict arises that is *not* merely a matter of understanding, cooperation, or compromise. For example, we may be confronted with an action, behavior, or attitude that actually causes harm. We may be faced with a mythology that goes against our own set of ethics or values. For example, we may be asked to do something at work that we feel is wrong, or we may feel pressured to express views our family members or friends hold, even when we deeply disagree with them.

These situations reflect basic differences in mythology, ethics, and values. They present us with *dilemmas*—choices between our worldview and someone else's. When we can't *live and let live,* when a choice must be made, when compromise or cooperation won't solve the problem, we have to take a stand. We have to support ourselves, and back up our beliefs and views with action. It's impossible to live a completely value-free life—at some time or another, we must each decide what we believe to be *wrong.*

Once we have examined ourselves and discovered ways *we* may cause harm to others, we can begin to understand the fears, confusion, and self-doubt that motivate others to cause harm. Without being judgmental, we can see the errors in their choices and underlying mythologies. We can choose to take a stand against the harm and refuse to participate in it.

Turning-Point Choices

This refusal is often a momentous occasion for us, a turning point in our lives and relationships. For example, one woman stopped accepting physical and emotional abuse from her husband and left him. A man says he left a lucrative job because he felt he had to be dishonest with his clients in order to keep it. Our moment of refusal may take many forms. Here are some common turning-point choices people have made:

I will not accept abuse.

I will not let my fears stop me from succeeding.

I will not let others tell me who I am.

I will not give in to an old negative self-image.

I will not fail in order to please others or fulfill their beliefs about me.

I will not participate in harming the environment, other people, or animals.

I will not let my family or in-laws run my marriage.

I will not allow my children to be harmed.

I will not do this dishonest / illegal / immoral thing at work.

Without Violence

Ordinarily, we think of a warrior as one who confronts "dragons," stands and fights, and slays them. The *peaceful* warrior does so without violence of any kind. Sometimes the dragon is our own fear of saying no, of standing up for what we believe in. The peaceful warrior doesn't harm our self-esteem with recriminations for our fear but gives us the courage to take a stand *in spite of it*. As a peaceful warrior, we don't have to harm the other person's self-image either, but we choose to disagree and refuse to participate in anything we believe is wrong or harmful.

Assertiveness is not the same as aggressiveness. We can take a stand against anything we feel is wrong and stand up for that which we believe to be right. But harming ourselves or others is never the way of the peaceful warrior and only harms everyone in the end. There are times in our lives when we are called on to take a stand, to bring our personal mythologies out through actions. We don't always have to agree with others, and we don't have to fall into old patterns. We can *consciously choose* our own personal view and express it fully and fearlessly.

Past Versus Present

In long-term relationships, we inevitably encounter conflicts with one another as we each grow, change, and evolve. Whether in marriages, family relations, or friendships, these conflicts require us to confront, communicate, and work out our differences. Sometimes these changes create *little* bumps, twists, and turns in ourselves and our relationships—opportunities for getting to know each other better and to grow closer together. Other times they signal *major* shifts in our relationships or even their endings.

Brian and his friend David were college roommates twenty years ago. Brian says they "did everything together and thought the same way about everything." While they remained in close touch, Brian and David lived very different lives over the years after leaving school.

Brian explains, "David spent a lot of the past twenty years addicted to alcohol. He was walking around, talking and everything, but he wasn't really *there*. Now that he's gotten treatment and has been sober for a while, I feel like he went into a coma when he was about twenty, and he's just now coming out of it. Sometimes I'll start talking to him about something that happened five or ten years ago, and then I realize that *he doesn't remember it at all*. It may have been real important to me, but for him it didn't even happen. I know he can't help it, but it's strange for me to have this shared history with someone who doesn't even remember any of it.

"I love David," Brian continues, "and I'm happy that he has literally started his life over again. It's the best thing that could have happened for him, and I wish him well. But the thing is, I'm just not back there with him—twenty years ago, just starting a career, taking responsibility for his money for the first time, falling in love, planning to get married. The things that are uppermost in my mind now are being a good father, paying off my mortgage, putting my kids through college, deciding about making a midlife career move, and continuing to work on my relationship with my wife after twenty years of marriage. Our viewpoints are completely different now."

Common Wisdom

Brian's story reflects a conflict between his current mythology and the one he shared with his friend a long time ago. Common wisdom says that you can't go home again, and this is the reason why—our personal mythology at any point in the past can never completely match our current one. Depending on many factors, our worldview changes a little or a lot over time, but it always changes. David has also changed, although not in the same ways as Brian. The conflict between our past and present mythologies reflects the conflict between our past and present selves.

CONFLICTS WITHIN OURSELVES

As we evolve through our lives, we encounter conflicts within ourselves. Each stage of our personal growth and development has its own belief system, and each must stretch and change as we move into other stages. At each stage of our development, different priorities and problems form our personal mythology. Different questions need to be answered.

New experiences always broaden our worldview, challenging our old one. Taking courses, going away to college, traveling or moving to new places, starting a new job, and meeting new people all inspire reevaluation. Each time we are confronted with anything new, whether it's a new feeling or idea inside us or a new circumstance outside us, we have to stretch in some way to accommodate it. We're all doing this all the time, even if we're not aware of it. Becoming conscious of these processes can help facilitate them.

A Model of Changing Mythology

We don't change our mythology overnight. Growth from one worldview to another is a *process,* a series of stages through which we gradually evolve. In their book, *Personal Mythology,* authors David Feinstein and Stanley Krippner identify five stages of growth through a changing mythology: Old Myth, Counter-Myth, Unifying Vision, Commitment, and New Myth.

In the first stage of this model, our *old mythology* starts giving us trouble. It doesn't fulfill the functions for which we need it. When we realize that our old mythology can't work for us anymore, we often swing over to the *opposite viewpoint*. Since this new myth is a *reaction* to the old myth, it doesn't completely serve as our new worldview, but helps us break out of the old one. In the third stage, we begin sifting through all the aspects of both views, consciously choosing to keep some and reject others. We develop a *vision* which takes into account elements of both the old myth and the counter-myth. Next, we *commit* to this new mythology by facing and resolving the inevitable conflicts that arise as the two views struggle into a new, third form.

Finally, the *new mythology* becomes a natural part of our daily life. The struggles have been resolved, and we arrive at a new worldview. This new viewpoint is reflected in our beliefs, attitudes, and actions. While remnants of the old conflicts may reappear from time to time, as familiar choices are replaced by unfamiliar ones, the new mythology is firmly in place—until we outgrow it.

We can use this structure to help us clarify our own passages through our various mythologies. It may take hours, days, weeks, or even years for us to go through the five stages of changing our mythologies. We're going through them all the time, evolving various aspects of our worldview at various rates.

We will always need to keep letting our worldview or mythology change, grow, and evolve. Our openness to continued renewal keeps our guiding mythology alive, growing, and serving us in the best ways possible. We need not fear or avoid conflict within ourselves. It's an opportunity for enlarging our worldview, evolving our mythology. It's the doorway to personal growth.

Setting Our Priorities

Personal growth and ever-changing circumstances create a series of conflicting mythologies for us to face and reconcile within ourselves. But there may also be conflicts between various aspects of our mythological worldview at any particular time.

For example, our mythology may include a strong belief that earning money to support our family is a value. On the other hand, it may also value ethical, honest work that uses our talents and doesn't keep us away from our family too much of the time. These values may at times conflict with each other. We may be required to do something at work we don't feel quite right about, or we may be expected to spend so many hours on the job that we neglect our family in other ways.

When these kinds of conflicts arise, we need to clarify the underlying mythologies and *set our priorities*. We can consider both the short-term and long-term consequences of our choices. We can examine the aspects of our mythology that we take for granted, to see whether we really have more options than we thought. There is no set, easy answer for all of these dilemmas. They must be faced individually, taking into account all the unique factors of the situation, place, time, and people involved.

For example, when we are raising children, our values

and priorities are different than when we are childless. And having small children requires different priorities than we'll have when our children are older. While putting our children through college, salary may be the most important aspect of our job choices. Our priorities change continually as our life circumstances change. We can look at these dilemmas clearly, examine all aspects of our mythologies, and make the best choices for us right now.

Is Your Mythology Too Small?

Conflicts are inevitable. There are as many viewpoints as there are people on this planet. The smaller and more rigid our mythological worldview, the more conflicts we'll confront and the more difficult they will be to resolve. If our mythology isn't large enough to allow for diversity, change, and growth, it isn't large enough for human life.

Conflicts with others are opportunities to find common ground, mutual goals, complementary viewpoints, and abilities to cooperate. Conflicts within ourselves are chances to learn, grow, and understand more. Both types of conflict are signals to reexamine, expand, and update our worldview. We can face all the conflicts our mythologies encounter with self-awareness, empathy, flexibility, openness, and acceptance. We can take a stand when it's necessary, peacefully asserting our best selves. We can let go of old aspects of our mythology that no longer work for us and grow into new ones that are as large as life itself.

EXERCISES

Trading Places

Think about a conflict you're having with someone in your life. Imagine you are that person. How does it feel to be in his or her position? Can you see the situation from that perspective? What can you learn from this? How does it change your own perspective?

Change and Growth

Examine a change you've already been through in terms of the five-stage model described, which begins on page 59. This can be a religious, political, or personal viewpoint, attitude, or belief you've outgrown. Trace your growth through the Old Myth, Counter-Myth, Unifying Vision, Commitment, and New Myth stages. Now choose a conflict you're facing in your current relationships or inner life. Where are you in the process? What stages have you been through and resolved? Where do you need to go from here?

CHAPTER FOUR

New Personal Myths

*Man is the being which is capable of creating symbols,
and a being in need of symbols.*

—VIKTOR FRANKL

When we have examined and rejected or outgrown
some aspects of our personal mythology, we can begin
creating new myths, parables, and metaphors to fulfill
our current needs. We can look back over the stories of
our life and interpret them in new ways. We can consciously choose our personal mythology and create
effective ways to symbolize and ritualize it in our lives.

In the last chapter, we talked about taking a stand,
choosing what we will not do or accept. Now we can
look at these refusals from a positive viewpoint: *I will not
. . .* can now become *I will. . . .* Each old myth that is no
longer serving us can be replaced by a new one. This is
a chapter to do rather than just read. We have uncovered
old myths, interpretations, and perceptions of the world
through these chapters. Now is the time to let them go
and use our personal power to create new ones.

OLD MYTHS—NEW MYTHS

Our old worldview is composed of many aspects,
beliefs, or myths. Each one of these myths can be

65

examined for its effects on us and replaced, if we wish. We can begin by listing basic beliefs and aspects of our worldview, such as

> *I'm always screwing up.*
> *People will always hurt you in the end.*
> *Love means hearts, flowers, romance, and having someone do whatever I want them to do.*
> *Blood is thicker than water.*
> *I'm unlucky.*
> *I need others to rescue me.*
> *If it feels good, it's bad; if it hurts, it's good for me.*
> *Everyone has to agree with me.*
> *Anger always means violence or abandonment.*
> *I have to please my family.*

This list could go on forever. Make a list of some myths you think are hindering your ability to live a full, happy, successful life. Now take each one and think of a corresponding statement to replace it. Your new myth should be positive, helpful, and something you can really believe in. Work at this a little, writing and rewriting your new myths.

For example, *I'm always screwing up* can become *Nobody's perfect,* or *Sometimes I make mistakes,* or *I learn from my mistakes.* We can think about some of the specific ways in which we've "screwed up" and begin to see them in a new light. Maybe they weren't really so bad, or maybe we've already made amends for them or we now see ways we could make appropriate amends. Maybe we learned something important from the experiences we couldn't have learned any other way. Or maybe we were simply assigned the role of *the family screw-up* and integrated that into our self-image. In any case, we can now recognize this bit of our overall worldview and replace it with something better.

Examining Our Myths

We can thoroughly examine each myth for its source, effects, and possible replacement from our individual viewpoint. Here are a few examples of new myths that could replace the ones listed on page 66. We can use these lists as a starting point to get into our own personal self-examination.

People will always hurt you can become *Some people can be trusted and others can't; I sometimes feel hurt by other people's choices; I will be all right, anyway;* or *Relationships can be wonderful, loving experiences.*

Blood is thicker than water can be replaced by *I love my family, but they aren't always right; I don't always have to please them or agree with them;* or *I deserve to be treated with respect and love by those close to me.*

I'm unlucky can become *Sometimes things go wrong, and sometimes things go well; I'm okay whatever happens.*

Everyone has to agree with me can change to *Everyone has a different point of view; Live and let live; I'm not threatened by anyone else's opinion;* or *I can learn a lot from various viewpoints.*

We can work through our myths—from old unhelpful ones to new, brief, simple, and positive statements. Your personal myths are of your own choosing. Take the time to choose them *consciously,* and they can serve to help you, heal you, guide you, and bring out the best in you and in your life's potential.

Old Stories—New Interpretations

We've talked a lot about all the stories of our lives and how we may have derived parables, myths, and beliefs from them. Now we can look back over these stories from our new vantage point and reinterpret them. We can choose a new moral to the stories, pick a different angle to emphasize or a different meaning to assign them. No viewpoint or perception is ever carved in stone—we can always change our minds about old stories and our interpretations of them.

For example, in Chapter One we heard from Zina, whose parents left their work in an opera company to raise her. Zina said she grew up feeling responsible for taking away something from her parents that they had loved. But as an adult, Zina now realizes that her parents made their own decisions, that she was never responsible for their happiness, and that they love her and never blamed her or felt they'd made the wrong choice. Her old interpretation of her parents' stories of their days in the opera company has now given way to a new, more mature viewpoint and relationship with her parents.

Carla stopped writing when other people read her diary. Having her privacy invaded and trust betrayed left Carla feeling vulnerable and unable to express herself freely. But her desire to write and years of experiences with other friends who didn't violate her privacy enabled Carla to outgrow that part of her mythology. Carla now says she has learned to expect her privacy to be respected, and also to stop making broad generalizations from every individual experience. Just because someone does something one time, it doesn't mean *everyone* will *always* do the same.

You can think back over your own life stories. If you did the exercises in the earlier chapters, you will have plenty of material to work with. You can now look at these old stories and the morals you've assigned them from a new perspective.

Fictional Stories

As we grow in reinterpreting the stories of our past, we can also look back on the fairy tales, movies, and other stories in our lives. We can examine our past interpretations of these stories, and choose a new viewpoint. Critics, reviewers, and teachers do not have the last word on what *we* can glean from these tales. There is never only one "right" way to look at any story. Exposure to many viewpoints can help us broaden our own, but learning to rigidly interpret everything from someone else's viewpoint only stunts our own personal growth and narrows our mythology.

Our interpretations always come from within us—and that's just as true for everyone else, including people who write stories and make movies and those who review them.

Let Our Imaginations Go

To exercise our creativity and stretch our personal mythology, we can try looking at a story from as many viewpoints as possible. We can really let our imaginations go with this. We can choose the points of view of different characters in the story. Even the villain, the shrew, and Ebenezer Scrooge have their stories too. We can ask ourselves how they got this way and why they're so unhappy. We can examine the story from an ethical, political, religious, scientific, or psychological viewpoint. We can imagine the story as seen through the eyes of a child, adolescent, adult, or older person.

Another exercise could be to learn one interpretation from a class or reviewer and then deliberately try to reinterpret the story in a different way. Imagine the opposite of whatever the "expert" perceptions are. Or take the main symbolism of the story and change it to something completely different. Ask yourself: *What if this "love story" is really a political message? What if there's a positive message in this apparently negative story—what could it be? What if this shark is a symbol for evil in the world or the mysterious, unknown side of ourselves, or just a shark doing what sharks naturally do?*

Such exercises can help us break out of the old perspective that there always has to be one right answer. *There are always many ways to look at anything.* We can practice these kinds of exercises often to help us avoid getting stuck in one narrow viewpoint and to keep our personal mythology alive and growing.

The way we view and understand any story is also different at different times in our lives. As our personal mythology changes, so does our interpretation of everything around us. We can look back now and reexamine old books, movies, and stories of all kinds that were important or interesting to us at another time. This can provide us with some clues about our own development.

As our mythology gets larger and more mature, we can see so much more in everything we look at. Layers and levels of interpretation become clearer as we grow in our understanding of many viewpoints. All our old stories can now lead us to new insights and perceptions.

SYMBOLS AND RITUALS

Since the beginning of recorded history, we have created symbols and rituals to reflect our beliefs and guide or structure our lives. We've used them to celebrate and to mourn, to honor and to punish. We've depended on them to provide predictable, familiar rites for births, deaths, weddings, graduations, and other important life events. We've used them to give meaning to our lives.

Symbols

Native American headdresses, necklaces, and other ornaments worn on the body symbolize the accomplishments of the wearer. From Hawaiian hula skirts to the black veils of Muslim women, people all over the world still wear many symbolic costumes. But such symbolic adornments are not limited to the exotic clothing of faraway peoples. Think of the many symbols reflected in everyday Western wear: wedding dresses and rings, graduation caps and gowns, funeral and mourning black, religious habits, serving uniforms, class rings, sorority and fraternity pins, lab coats, military uniforms and medals, business suits, gold watches, and designer labels.

Cars, homes, furniture, and appliances; boats, bikes, and other sports equipment have all developed symbolic meaning in our culture. Meals can reflect everything from family togetherness to high-fashion snobbery. A rabbit's foot, a four-leaf clover, or a ribbon tied around the leg of a baby's crib can represent our superstitions.

The flags we fly everywhere and the national anthem we sing before every ball game signify our patriotism. When we really look, we find ourselves surrounded by symbolic objects and constantly participating in symbolic events.

Rituals

Thus steeped in symbolism, we find comfort in what could otherwise be seen as a chaotic world. Events are given structure and meaning. We know what to do when someone is born, dies, moves, marries, or graduates. We hold house-warming parties, periodic reunions, and ground-breaking, ribbon-cutting, and mortgage-burning ceremonies.

While our culture, religions, families, schools, and other established institutions provide us with many of these ceremonies, rituals, and symbols, we also make up many of our own. We record our children's first steps and words. We plant our handprints in the wet cement of our new driveway or patio. We savor our first night in a new home, and reminisce on our last night in an old one. We photograph *everything*. We find ways to stop and say, *This is special*.

These symbols, ceremonies, and rituals are important to mark the significant occasions and passages in our lives. If we don't celebrate the events that are important to us, we're robbing ourselves of the joy we could find in everyday life. We're not allowing ourselves to experience our own lives fully.

Phil says his family stopped celebrating his birthdays when he reached adolescence. "Birthdays were just for little kids," he explains. "After about twelve or so, my birthdays were just nothing special. I'd get maybe one small present, and everyone in my family would say 'Happy Birthday,' and that was it."

Phil says he didn't think he was missing anything until after he got married. "My wife makes a big deal about birthdays, holidays, all that stuff," he explains. "She really goes in for all that—cake, ice cream, flowers, balloons, presents, parties, and going out. She does it for me and our kids, and I know she'll keep doing it as the kids get older. She always says, *If your own parents don't celebrate the day you were born, who will?* And I admit that I like it—being fussed over like that one day a year. It makes me feel special and loved and part of a family. It's fun."

Celebrate

The day you were born is a wonderful, special day for you. Celebrate it! Even if no one else does, make it a birthday present to yourself. Take the day off work, get your hair done, go out for a meal or to a movie or ball game or whatever you enjoy—*have fun*. Give yourself flowers, balloons, or a cake. It's the only holiday of the year just for *you*. You deserve to celebrate it.

There are many other special events in our lives that just slip away into the past if we aren't careful. All we have to do is become aware of them, savor them, and appreciate them. When you achieve a goal, *celebrate*. When you lose something you valued, allow yourself to mourn. Symbolize your beginnings, endings, transitions, and changes of all kinds. Cleanse yourself of the old in preparation for the new. These symbolic rituals help us clearly identify each step of our life's journey and avoid slipping back into past viewpoints and behaviors.

Earlier, Mary told us of her second wedding to symbolize a new era in her relationship with her husband. Our symbolic acts can be as elaborate as a wedding ceremony or as simple as a handshake. We can stop and take a moment to celebrate our last payment on a loan, dedicate a freshly painted room, or say goodbye to the old family car. We can give thanks for the harvest from our garden or give our dead goldfish a proper funeral.

Mark the occasions of your life with your own little ceremonies, rituals, and symbols. Some of these can be private moments of self-care, and some can be shared with other people. Whether it's an Alcoholics Anonymous anniversary medal or a second honeymoon, your symbols and rituals are important and enrich your experience of life.

MANDALAS

A mandala is a circle that symbolizes *you*—your worldview, mythology, and self-image. Few of us have family crests or shields these days, symbolizing our family's heritage. Our mandala is our personal shield or crest, representing all the aspects of our personal mythology. We can use this symbol to help us clarify our self-image and worldview and to keep track of our changing mythology.

Draw a large circle on a sheet of paper. Divide the circle into sections, like a pie. Now label each section with aspects of yourself and your life, such as *Family, Work, Marriage, School,* and any other important areas of your life. In each section, list your accomplishments and strengths for that area. Fill out your mandala until you feel it reflects you accurately right now. If you wish, you can make several mandalas: one focusing on your past, one on your present, and another on the things you want to work on or improve.

Another way of looking at a mandala is as a *wheel of fortune.* Around the outside of the wheel are the outward manifestations of our lives—the circumstances and feelings that are always going up or down. But in the hub of the wheel is a calm fixed center. We can use the mandala to help us explore the various aspects of ourselves and find our own unchanging center. This revelation can help us find peace, calm, and a solid foundation within ourselves no matter how things seem to go up and down in our lives.

One more way we can use the mandala is to divide it into four equal parts, representing our body, mind, heart, and soul. We can categorize all the aspects of our lives and selves under these four headings. This can help us to recognize areas we may have been neglecting and to find clarity and balance in our lives.

We can keep a notebook of our mandala drawings or draw them in our journals. Mandala drawings can be especially helpful for people who don't like to write in journals, as they can quickly and simply represent what may otherwise take pages and pages of writing to express. We can date and check our mandalas periodically to update our personal mythology and record our accomplishments and development.

TOWARD OUR NEW MYTHOLOGY

The day never comes when our personal mythology no longer requires reexamination and revision. As long as we are alive, our mythology is alive and growing too. Taking care to consciously examine and stretch our worldview as we move along the pathway of our life keeps us balanced between the old and the new, the past and the future.

We can now claim our power to choose our own mythological worldview. We can examine every aspect of our beliefs, assumptions, and actions to discover their underlying myths. We can let go of old myths that no longer serve our best interests and choose new ones that can help us move into our own best future. We can recall old stories and view them through fresh eyes. We can fill our lives with symbols and rituals that accurately express our true selves and fulfill our true needs.

Claiming Our Power

In Chapter Three, I said that self-examination always comes first. We must truly know ourselves, understand ourselves, and claim our own power to learn, grow, and choose our mythology before we can begin truly understanding, caring about, and helping others. Now is the time to turn outward. The fourth chakra of compassion teaches us that we are all interconnected beings, part of many larger communities and one whole world.

Now that we have found ourselves, we can begin finding each other. Now that we understand ourselves better as individuals, we can begin understanding ourselves better together. Now that we've learned to exercise our personal power to change our worldview, we can begin exploring our collective power to change our world.

CHAPTER FIVE

Our Need to Belong

*The need for social approval is as fundamental
to the human animal as the need for food.*
—SAM KEEN AND ANNE VALLEY-FOX

We all want to be accepted and approved of by other
people around us. We seek comradeship to avoid isola-
tion, fear, self-doubt, and perceived dangers. We form
our self-identity, at least in part, based on the groups to
which we belong.

From our earliest experiences, we learn to see ourselves as part of a wide variety of groups or communities: family, religion, race, gender, citizenship, ethnicity,
and social class or economic level, to name a few. Our
place in some of these groups is assured by birth; in
others, we learn to maintain our position by conforming
to certain rules of behavior.

As we grow older and more independent, we find
many ways to satisfy our need for belonging. We join
all kinds of clubs and form all kinds of groups—religious, political, social, and professional. We get together with others for a common purpose whenever we
possibly can. Whether the purpose is to raise money for
charity, share our problems and triumphs in Twelve
Step meetings, promote a political cause, root for the

home team, sew a quilt, celebrate, or just relax, we join together for the feeling of being *not alone.*

WHAT OUR GROUPS CAN DO FOR US

The human need to belong drives us to marry and form families, schools, religions, professions, sports teams, neighborhoods, towns and cities, nations, and all kinds of social and support groups. It provides us with emotional support, spiritual guidance, health care, education, companionship, and a sense of identity. It serves us in these and in other capacities to fulfill many of our most important needs as human beings.

When we join with others, we may derive many benefits from our participation. Together, we can accomplish things we never could alone. We find and create collective meanings and purposes in life. We structure our social behavior for the good of the many. We learn teamwork and cooperation, and develop our ability to help one another.

Community building means drawing many unique individuals together for a common purpose. Each individual is needed to contribute his or her special abilities, insights, and energy. Whether our purpose is to run a government, clean up our environment, eliminate poverty and hunger, find cures for diseases, or fight a common enemy, we can achieve much more together than each of us could alone.

Cultural Traditions

Throughout history, we have achieved and advanced through our collective, cooperative efforts. The diverse cultures of the world have made countless contributions to all of us, in every area of life from medicine to agriculture, art, science, and spiritual teachings. Humanity is a vast interconnected family, needing each group to make its unique contribution.

Belonging to a group can give us a rich sense of following tradition, carrying on something of value for all humankind. Hmong families who relocated from Southeast Asia to America continue to practice and teach their traditional arts and crafts, despite the devastation of war in their homeland. Native Americans teach us a great deal about reverence for the earth, in a time when our industrialization has caused so much damage to the natural environment. From each diverse tradition, we can glean teachings, practices, and different viewpoints to help and enrich us all.

The sense of tradition we can derive from our cultures can also fulfill a personal need to find our place in historical context and global connectedness. Feeling that we are part of something much larger than ourselves can infuse our lives with purpose and meaning. Bringing what is valuable from the past and preserving it for the future or contributing our bit to a long continuum of human endeavor can elevate our activities beyond present concerns.

Personal Rewards

Individually, our need to belong can help us find and use our own talents, intelligence, and creativity in ways that benefit others. It can give us the self-esteem that comes from effective, contributive social living. It can fulfill our own needs and the needs of others in an interconnected harmony. It can help bring out the best that is in each of us.

Our groups help us make sense of the world, share meaning with others, and find support when we feel confused or alone. We may eventually sort through and reject some aspects of the cultural worldviews we are taught, but they give us a starting place to begin examining ourselves and our world. As children, we generally accept whatever cultural paradigm we're born into. As we grow older, we begin choosing other groups and worldviews to embrace or reject. We balance the influences around and inside us.

Belonging to a group also helps us feel protected from possible disaster. Whether that disaster comes in the form of human enemies, forces of nature, accidents, disease, hunger, or poverty, we want to feel there will be help available to us if and when we need it. Together, we humans have survived all this time, and, together, we feel we can continue to survive and flourish. Instinctively, we join together for our common good.

If a culture, society, or group satisfies our emotional need to belong, contributes to our well-being, and allows us to contribute in our unique way, it can survive as a good, healthy society. And we can survive, flourish, and grow as healthy members of the group.

WHAT OUR GROUPS CAN DO TO US

The dark side to our human need for belonging can be seen in repressive conformity and giving up our self-responsibility to others. A group may seem to provide security, comradeship, and group identity to emotionally needy members, but eventually prove self-destructive. Even seemingly innocuous groups, such as "mainstream" religious, social, professional, academic, and political organizations can limit our worldview to a repressive and possibly dangerous degree.

Blind and total conformity is always damaging to ourselves—our well-being and self-respect. But knee-jerk rebellion against conformity can be just as damaging. Both of these reactions are based on *fear*. Each of our basic human needs has a corresponding fear, and our need to belong involves fears of abandonment, rejection, loneliness, and ostracism. Whenever we allow these fears to take over our thinking and behavior, we give up our self-responsibility, freedom of choice, and ability to contribute positively to our communities.

Within our groups, we can't always see the mythology at work, affecting us and others. Everything and everyone around us may be so entrenched in the mythology that we lose sight of any alternatives. But prevailing myths are no excuse for going along with harmful beliefs and behavior. Just because everyone around us seems to take a certain view for granted doesn't mean we have to conform to unethical practices.

Alienation

Another problem our need to belong can create happens when we feel we don't quite fit into a group that we wish to belong to. We may feel tremendous self-doubt and even self-hate for failing to meet certain criteria. We may feel torn between being ourselves and belonging. We may feel afraid, insecure, defensive, and lonely. If our place in the group feels threatened, we may react by lashing out in anger, retreating into a self-protective shell, or trying to manipulate our way back into a secure position in the group, whatever it takes.

The opposite of belonging is *alienation*. Feeling alienated from others is a painful human condition. It can bring us deep sorrow, shame, and fearfulness. It can distort our view of ourselves, others, and the world. It can also make us vulnerable to the lure of groups that are destructive to our well-being.

If we grew up feeling disconnected from family, school, church, and community, we may desperately crave a sense of belonging. Without strong attachments in place, any suggestion of acceptance or comradeship may be irresistibly attractive to us. We may be willing to overlook, rationalize, or accept danger, abuse, or personal pain in exchange for that feeling of belonging to the group.

Examples of this kind of self-destructive group can include the religious cults or street gangs we hear so much about. But they can also include everyday relationships within marriages, families, workplaces, schools, friendships, or any other relationship. In healthy relationships and group memberships, we are not harmed. Belonging doesn't have to mean total conformity, suffering, or sacrifice. If it does, maybe we need to think about removing ourselves from the relationship or group.

We can always ask ourselves, *What is the price I have to pay to belong?* If we must give up our self-responsibility or our well-being, it isn't worth it. Belonging to groups that recognize our humanity and enhance our well-being can enrich our lives. But giving up our true selves for membership in any group is a drastically uneven trade and can only harm us.

Stereotypes and Assumptions

Our need to belong can also prove harmful if we use it to stereotype others and separate ourselves from them. Rigidly grouping and categorizing ourselves and others prevents us from growing in understanding and acceptance of each other. For example, if we're having trouble with our in-laws, declaring that "no one gets along with in-laws" won't help the situation. In fact, it will close the door to any possibility of true communication and working through our differences.

Broad generalizations about groups of people build walls, not bridges, between us. We can't really get to know individuals if all we can see when we look at them are stereotypical assumptions. We can't respect and honor them as every human being deserves if we see them as caricatures rather than real, whole people.

We may have learned many stereotypical beliefs and views over the years without realizing it. Some of these assumptions may limit our worldview and harm our ability to relate to others and live effectively in the world. Following are some examples of statements people have made and common stereotypical assumptions:

Wealthy people are smarter, nicer, or better than others.
Poor people are lazy, stupid, or bad.
Older people are weird, wise, or useless.
Young people are selfish, rebellious, carefree, igno-rant, or untrustworthy.
People who dress well are rich, smart, honest, sincere, or trustworthy.

>*People who didn't go to college are lazy, ignorant, or
>   stupid.*
>*People who went to college are more liberal.*

When we begin listing all the stereotypes and
assumptions we're so used to hearing and making, we
realize just how vast and pervasive this habit of general-
izing and stereotyping really is. We can see these
stereotypes in movies, television shows, advertising,
and all other forms of mass media. When a newscaster
informs us that a disease or social problem cuts across
all socioeconomic lines, the clear implication is that we
would naturally have presumed otherwise. We're
expected to be surprised when a minister gets caught in
a sex scandal, or a lawyer turns out to be sensitive,
honest, and fair.

We hear a lot about "negative stereotyping," but I
have a hard time trying to imagine *positive* stereotyping.
Stereotypes are stereotypes—they're judgments or
assumptions we make about persons based on the
groups to which they belong, or about whole groups
based on the actions of one member. *Ministers are perfect* makes no more sense than *Lawyers are cutthroat
cheats*. Whatever the assumption or judgment, making
it cuts us off from real communication with one another
and reduces others and ourselves to false images rather
than real, whole human beings.

There is a big difference between learning about
someone's cultural background in order to better understand that part of him or her and using that information
to make judgments and assumptions about that person.
A relationship is a complex dynamic involving many
levels—personal, cultural, and universally human—of

the individuals in it. Failure to recognize and respect each other as full human beings blocks our relationships. We'll never stop fighting, distrusting, and hurting each other until we stop insisting on viewing one another as anything less than fully human.

Recognizing our cultural diversity and people's various mythologies can help us understand one another and communicate better. We can use a cultural perspective to either label, generalize, blame, judge, and make assumptions about each other, or we can use it to broaden our perspective and build true communication between us. The choice is always ours to make.

COLLECTIVE RESPONSIBILITY

Rigidly defining our own and other groups also cuts off our self-responsibility and contributive power in the community. For example, if we feel our group is powerless or victimized in society, this belief may become an excuse for destructive or self-destructive behavior, or simply refusing to participate in efforts for positive change.

This may explain at least one reason so many eligible American voters don't turn out for elections—and then complain about the results of those contests. Or perhaps we don't bother recycling or being careful about the products we use and throw away because we believe our behavior isn't that important in the larger scheme of things. Turning over our personal power to a cultural myth is throwing away our self-responsibility and the potential contributions we could make to our larger groups.

There was a time in recent history when, as a woman, I would not have enjoyed many of the rights, freedoms, and opportunities I now take for granted. But if women of that earlier day had not been willing to point out the inequities and need for social change, we today would not have the benefits of their contributions. *We are* all *responsible for the character of the groups and society in which we live.* Our communities need our contributions to keep them alive and growing and to make them the best that they can be.

Finding a Balance

Our need to belong is natural and healthy and can have many positive effects in our lives and communities. We can avoid the pitfalls by balancing our individual and cultural identities and remembering that we must bring to our communities our whole healthy selves.

We are all members of larger groups and communities, but that is only one aspect of our total selves. None of us is a stereotyped image of any group. We are all complex human beings. When we recognize our own and each other's humanity, as well as the cultural effects at work on us, we can use this broader view to understand ourselves and one another better.

Individualism is a big part of the American mythology. In some ways, this may help us achieve our unique potential. In other ways, it separates and isolates us from one another. When we learn to balance our collective and individual responsibilities and identities, we can fulfill our need to belong and to be fully ourselves at the same time. We need our communities, and our communities need us—to give and take in a harmonious, interconnected web of healthy whole individuals.

EXERCISES

Belonging

List all the groups to which you belong. Which ones have you no choice about? Which ones have you chosen? Why?

How does belonging to each group help you? In what ways does it harm you? What contributions do you make in each group?

Stereotypes and Assumptions

What *stereotypes and assumptions* do other people make about members of your groups? How do you fit the stereotypes? How don't you fit them? What stereotypes and assumptions do you make about other groups? Find examples that don't fit your preconceived ideas.

CHAPTER SIX

Reflections of Our Cultures

*Cultural norms and mores are the great unexamined
assumptions that run our lives.*

—MARILYN FERGUSON

Each of our groups or cultures has its own set of
beliefs, values, priorities, goals, accepted behaviors, and
taboos—its own worldview or mythology. This mythology is taught and expressed in the culture's language,
art, rituals, customs, and institutions. We need only look
as far as popular music, visual art, advertising, books,
magazines, movies, and television to get a clear picture
of current American culture—as confused and contra-
dictory as that mythology may be.

There are also many other groups and cultures func-
tioning within the context of American society. We
don't use the word "subculture" anymore, because part
of the American democratic mythology says that all cultures are equal and the prefix "sub-" implies that some
groups are *beneath* others. These various cultures may
compete or conflict with one another in both our inner
and outer worlds.

No one belongs to, or is affected by, only one culture
or group. Doing the exercises in the previous chapter,

we listed the many groups to which we belong. Each of these groups has its own mythology, affecting our beliefs, behaviors, and lives in a variety of ways.

Mei-Ying was born and lived in pre-Communist China until the age of nine. She says she escaped the sexism of traditional Chinese culture because her mother died when she was less than one year old and her father raised her. Mei-Ying explains, "The traditional Chinese mother and grandmother would teach the girls a kind of quiet stoicism that was the place of traditional Chinese women. I was always free to express my thoughts and feelings with my father, and he made me feel there was nothing that I couldn't do because I was a girl."

Mei-Ying did grow up with many other aspects of traditional Chinese thought and culture. "Chinese thinking is a combination of Confucianism, Taoism, and Buddhism," she says.

Confucianism

Mei Ying explains: "Confucianism is a philosophy that gives you a code of ethics and conduct to deal with your relationships. It's a very clear-cut set of rules, very structured. There is no confusion—every relationship has a specific set of duties and obligations on both sides. You don't have to choose or figure anything out; you always know how to conduct yourself in your dealings with others."

Taoism

While many people think of Taoism as a religion, Mei-Ying says it really isn't one. "Taoism doesn't talk about anything before or after this life," she explains. "It is simply about your relationship with nature. It teaches *harmony* with nature, that nature is good, and we shouldn't aggressively resist it. When something happens that seems bad, you have to look for the speck of good in it. You have to be patient, because time will turn that bad thing into good. The symbols of *yin* and *yang* express this. You need two opposites—both the bad and the good, the dark and the light—to make a whole. The dark side of the symbol has a spot of light and the light side has a spot of darkness. It's all part of one harmonious whole. But you have to be patient and let nature go through the cycles it needs to go through."

Buddhism

Mei-Ying says Buddhism isn't really Chinese, but was imported from India. "In fact," she tells us, "there has never been a religion born in China. Taoism and Confucianism are really philosophies of life. But Buddhism teaches that your spirit lives on again and again. You have to work through the suffering of this life until you perfect yourself and then you no longer have to live. Buddhism teaches that life is suffering, being is suffering, and *nirvana* is nonbeing, peace, no more need for suffering. It also goes along with the responsibilities taught in both Confucianism and Taoism, because whatever you do will affect future generations."

These three teachings—Confucianism, Taoism, and Buddhism—formed the basis for the Chinese thought and culture in which Mei-Ying grew up. She says, "They're used to tell you how to live and also to *explain life*. Traditional Chinese people aren't stressed out by all kinds of questions and choices."

She explains that these strong values still affect her life today in concrete ways. "I've been a teacher for twenty-five years, and even though I've had many opportunities to do other things, I never could accept them," she says. "In China, teaching is the highest, noblest profession. Teachers and government officials are the most revered because they serve the public.

"China is an agricultural society, so farmers are second in line. Then come laborers and factory workers. Businessmen are at the lowest position. Making money on money is considered ignoble. Perhaps this is why I have felt guilty for even considering any job offers that would have been very lucrative for me."

Mei-Ying describes the most startling experience of her early years in America—her first encounter with an American family. She had been invited to spend a weekend at the home of one of her classmates. When the family disagreed about which movie to go see after dinner, a vote was taken and the majority made the choice. Mei-Ying says, "Even the youngest of the six children in the family had an equal vote with the older ones and the parents. This was absolutely the most astounding thing in the world to me! In traditional Chinese society, the father figure made up his mind what the family was going to do, and that was that. Everyone else followed along—you never questioned his authority or expected to have a say in the decisions."

A Societal Structure

Mei-Ying says this traditional family system reflected the entire societal structure. Emperors and other government officials were seen as "wise, benevolent leaders," entrusted with the decision-making power to guide and rule the people. Mei-Ying says that "a largely uneducated, illiterate population *required* this highly structured society, where everyone has a place, a position, and behaves accordingly."

China's recent influence from the West has created confusion and stress, Mei-Ying says. "Democracy must have the right conditions for it to grow. China is far from ready, far from having those conditions. China is too poor to share the way a democracy can share. A democracy requires an educated, informed population to elect its leaders. When you have such high illiteracy, how can the people read the name of the person they're voting for, never mind understanding what that person represents? It's like Taoism teaches—*harmony takes time*. China must go through many more cycles before opposites blend with each other and become something new."

CULTURES IN CONFLICT

Whoever we are, we all have stories like the one above. Imagine Native American children being taught in school that Columbus *discovered* America, when they know that their ancestors were already here; or Jewish children, inundated year after year with Christmas stories, songs, decorations, pageants, and activities.

It isn't only the more obvious ethnic and religious cultures that conflict. Many subtle cultural norms and mores affect our daily lives. Millions of Americans put on business suits five days a week and take on the beliefs, rituals, language, and values of the corporate world. Medicine, law enforcement, the military, and countless other fields of study and work have their own specific mythologies. Citizens of urban, suburban, and rural communities often have different worldviews. Wealthy, middle-class, low-income, and homeless people may see the world through unique sets of beliefs and values. Whether we live within cultures of ethnicity, gender, politics, economics, business, academia, religion, or whatever, these cultures often conflict.

Maybe there was once a time or place where a person could grow up safe and secure in one worldview and never encounter a conflicting one. But in today's world, with all the technology that lets us know what's happening on the other side of the world as it's happening, that kind of insulation just isn't possible. Mass communication gives us a window on various world mythologies.

We grow up bombarded on every side with conflicting viewpoints, beliefs, values, and choices. Many of our modern-day stresses may be the result of exposure to so many different cultures, value systems, or worldviews. Pressures to conform to one or another of these conflicting mythologies can cause tremendous confusion and anxiety.

It would take a great deal of time, thought, and study to sort through all the philosophies and worldviews available to us. Most of us just live with a certain level of confusion and stress. Even if we do take the time and make the effort to thoroughly research, analyze, and reflect upon all our various options, we usually don't end up agreeing totally with one viewpoint and disagreeing with all the others. We can agree and disagree with various elements of various views.

Diversity Within Us

On a personal level, we can reconcile the conflicting cultural views within us and between our inner voice and outer cultural pressures. We can choose those aspects of each view that we wish to keep, and let go of the rest. With understanding and tolerance, we can allow *yin* and *yang* to blend within us, forming a new, third view. Understanding many different cultures and worldviews can help us put our own into context. It can enable us to find common ground with others and choose the best elements of each opposing view.

Examining what author Marilyn Ferguson calls the "unexamined assumptions" of our lives—consciously, thoughtfully, and purposefully—can open our eyes to the guiding myths of our cultures and lives. We can learn that it's okay for our world to be full of different views. Opposites *can* blend together into a harmonious whole. Differences *can* be accepted and worked out. Balance can be achieved.

Diversity in Our Outer World

Conflicts between cultural viewpoints are also played out on a larger scale. Diverse gangs, political groups,

97

religions, races, and nations engage in warfare with one another all over the world. Science, religion, and art oppose one another as if they were not all addressing the same issues, simply using different metaphors. Countless cultural mythologies conflict and compete in the public arena. Even our "news" is never truly objective, but rather a reflection of cultural biases and values.

By simply recognizing this and becoming sensitive to the cultural myths underlying our interactions, we can begin overcoming their negative effects. We can choose those aspects of our various cultural mythologies that help us *connect* rather than separate from one another. We can hold on to the *ideals* of each worldview, rather than letting our human failings sour us on all ideology. With respect for the validity of every person's and group's mythology, we can discover the richness of diversity within our groups, nations, and world.

EXERCISES

Our Groups

Using your list of the various groups to which you belong, what are each group's specific *beliefs, values, priorities, goals, accepted behaviors,* and *taboos?* How are they expressed in the culture's language, art, entertainment, rituals, or institutions? How do your various cultures' mythologies differ from one another? In what ways are they similar?

Our Stories

Think about *stories from your own life* that illustrate the beliefs, values, and rules of each culture. Tell these stories to other people or write them down in your journal or a notebook.

Our Mythologies

In what ways have the mythologies of your groups affected you personally? How have they affected your relationships with others? How have they made you who you are now?

CHAPTER SEVEN

Cultural Evolution

All the evolution we know of proceeds from the vague to the definite.

—CHARLES SANDERS PEIRCE

No groups or cultures remain static and unchanging. They evolve through stages of growth and change, just as we individuals do. Cultural evolution is a long, slow process. Unlike *revolution,* which implies a sudden radical change to remedy social problems, cultural evolution is the broader, overall process of continuous social change. We revolt *against* something, we evolve *through* stages, *toward* something else. Revolution sounds easier than the sustained effort and patience needed for evolution. Evolution seems more difficult and takes longer—but it inevitably *works.* According to Taoism, which Mei-Ying described to us in the last chapter, it is the natural way of the universe. If we don't resist it, harmony is its eventual result.

In the short run, we always know more about what we're *against* than what we're *for.* Over time, we learn what we *are* and what we stand for by a gradual process of elimination. We figure out what works by learning about what does *not* work. We evolve "from the vague to the definite." Life—individually and collective-ly—is a trial and error process.

STAGES OF CULTURAL EVOLUTION

The same metaphors we've used to trace our individual development can be used to help us clarify and understand the cultural evolution of groups, nations, and the world. The hero's journey, the chakra ladder, stages of a life cycle, and a hierarchy of human needs can all be applied to cultural change.

These models can provide structures or frameworks on which to build a clearer understanding of our cultural history, just as we've learned to understand our personal history. And, just as we've learned to use that information to discover where we are in our individual development and where we want to go from here, we can begin to see the stages at which our groups and cultures now function and the directions in which we may want to help them go.

A Family Grows Through the Chakras

Using the chakra ladder—survival, sex, power, compassion, communication, knowledge, and enlightenment—let's look at the evolution of a hypothetical marriage. First, a young couple starts out together, coping with issues of survival—how they will make a living, buying basic necessities, setting up housekeeping. They develop an intimate relationship that evolves beyond the level of "honeymoon" romance. Over time, they grow to feel settled and secure in having resolved their basic survival and sex issues.

Issues of power soon emerge. Who does the house-work? Who manages the money and pays the bills? How are major decisions made? How are smaller, every-day decisions made? These and many other new issues in the relationship can create power struggles that are painful, confusing, and difficult for the couple. But they can be worked through, and harmonious adjustments and compromises reached.

When the couple has a child, both partners must face changes unlike anything they've experienced before. Suddenly, they are responsible for another human being—a tiny, helpless, dependent, wet, wailing, *beautiful* human being. Everything in the relationship needs to be reevaluated. Intimacy is interrupted by all the demands of the new little member of this group and the fatigue caused by meeting those demands. Work sched-ules, dining habits, social activity, and help from out-side the relationship all become important new problems to face. A huge amount of new expenses and purchases become necessary. And beneath all of these issues lies the most basic change that now these two people are *parents*.

Learning to Give

Parents must learn to give. Many of their own needs and desires must be bumped down their list of priori-ties. They must think about someone else besides them-selves all the time. They develop a compassionate ability to delay their own gratification in order to take care of their child. Issues involving children and fami-lies in general suddenly take on new meaning for them. They begin viewing many social problems and approaching many other people differently than they ever did before. Throughout this couple's child-rearing years, they grow in their ability to give, share, care, and empathize with others.

As this family evolves through time, many issues arise that can only be understood and resolved through communicating with one another. All the daily events and problems that exist in family life can be opportunities for developing open, honest, gentle, loving, clear communication that can benefit all the members and their relationships with each other. The family group also communicates with people and groups outside of itself. A public image is projected to the outer world—to schools, churches, businesses, and other communities and individuals.

Knowledge, in the context of this family illustration, can come from outside or inside the group. For example, new parents may read many books about babies and young children, or ask doctors, teachers, and other people for their knowledge and advice. They will also learn a great deal simply by living with their children. All through the years of family life, knowledge can be gained in both of these fashions, and both are valuable. With love, openness, and caring, the family can come to know about themselves, each other, and countless other things that can help them in every area of their lives.

A Family Evolves

Throughout this couple's lifetime together, many issues of survival, sex, power, compassion, communication, and knowledge will resurface to be faced, worked through, and resolved as this family group evolves. Children will grow up, relationships will change, people will come and go within the group, and, eventually, the family may bear little resemblance to the young couple who started out together all those years ago.

Does a family—or any group—ever reach the level of *enlightenment,* or perfection? Probably not. But there can come a day when this couple, having worked through many years of living together and raising a family, can realize how very much they've learned and grown through the experience, and how very valuable it has all been. As author Sam Keen has said, "True love—*unconditional* love—doesn't come at the beginning of a marriage. It comes at the end."

A Hero's Journey in Business

Our hero in this story could be any business, school, performing company, or group of that nature. A person or group of people start out with an idea or a product and set out to form a company or retail outlet. Along the way, many policies must be made and obstacles overcome. The group grows larger in number and more complex and specific in its identity. For example, a small group of people who like to dance can grow into a major performing company, with a large budget, rehearsal facilities, and contracts to fulfill. Or an individual selling a few bottles of homemade natural skin lotions can evolve into a multimillion dollar corporation.

At each step along this journey, there is a dragon to slay, an obstacle to overcome, or a change to incorporate into the growing company. Bank loans must be secured; space must be found for rehearsals, retail outlets, factories, or warehouses; partners and employees enter the picture; perhaps shares in the business are sold; franchise outlets are opened. Larger economic issues may affect the business, outside of its control. Hard times may come and go.

Other questions to be resolved involve the ethics and values that develop within the business. What are the company's goals, priorities, and guiding principles? What things will the company do and not do? What effects does the company have on the larger community? What public image will the company project? Over time, the company develops its own character, just as an individual does. Its manner of facing and dealing with all the dragons it encounters both creates and reflects the company's character.

A hero's journey has no clear end point—there is always another dragon to slay. The evolutionary steps don't always come in a predictable sequence of events and aren't always the same from one business to another. Both internal and external problems continually appear to be faced and resolved. The journey itself is the process of overcoming and resolving these problems, of perpetually perfecting the business or group.

Life Cycle of a Nation

The basic stages of childhood, adolescence, young adulthood, middle age, and old age can be applied to the history of a nation. As a country grows through stages of dependence, autonomy, initiative, and industry, it evolves into its unique identity. The intimacy that is the core issue for young adulthood can be reflected in development of compassion and cooperation among the people of a nation, both with each other and with other groups or nations.

The stage of generativity raises the next generation and leaves to it the legacy of its own social achievements and problems. This doesn't apply only to actual generations of people, but also eras of time. For example, the era of our nation's founding left many laws, ideas, and institutions we still have with us today. Though the people of our then-new nation lived several generations ago, their legacy still impacts us.

Each stage of this developmental evolution has its own corresponding myths. Mythology that is appropriate for a nation just building its economy will probably not be appropriate for a country that is older and more prosperous. The appropriate myths for an agricultural nation are not likely to work for an industrial or technological one. Old myths that no longer serve a community must fall away and be replaced by new myths for each of its new stages of cultural growth.

An Evaluation

Using the life cycle model, we can try to identify our nation's current stage of development. In his book *Voluntary Simplicity,* Duane Elgin writes, "We are in the adolescence of our evolution." And in her book *PragMagic,* Marilyn Ferguson writes of a study that calls the emerging cultural climate in the United States for the 1990s a "mid-life crisis of values."[*] Both the periods of adolescence and the mid-life point signal a reevaluation process, a shifting in old ways of thinking, and an

---

[*]SRI International Values and Lifestyles Study (VALS), 1989.

examination of our *identity*. It is often a period marked by upheaval, a time of making important changes.

Both of the authors quoted above were referring to current changes that are under way in our American mythology. But many more clear examples of such a cultural state of affairs can be seen in the important paradigm shifts evidenced by the reunification of Germany, the challenging of apartheid in South Africa, and the collapse of socialism in the former Soviet Union. Sometimes it's easier for us to see the changes in another group than it is to see the changes happening in our own society. But all groups and cultures can be thought of as growing through stages similar to the stages of growth in individual humans. Thinking this way about where nations might be in their development can help us see the underlying cultural mythologies and where they might be headed.

A Hierarchy of Global Needs

The needs of individuals cannot be separated from the needs of groups. Families, businesses, countries, and the whole world are made up of individual human beings. Meeting the needs of people is a primary concern for all groups and nations. When the basic needs of food, shelter, and health care are not being met in a community, it's hard for that community to evolve on to meeting the higher needs of its people. As long as people live under the imminent threat or even the possibility of war, their safety and security needs cannot be fully satisfied. Belonging needs cannot be met on a global level as long as countries, religions, and other groups of people vilify, hate, and fight one another.

Technology of travel and mass communication are fast making us one global community. The economic interdependence of countries is becoming more and more clear. The threats of environmental disaster and nuclear war affect every person on the earth. As long as the most basic survival and safety needs of people are not being met somewhere in the world, *the whole world is affected.* The more we neglect to resolve social problems, the more we threaten and fight one another, the more we hurt ourselves. Just as one individual must tend to the needs in all areas of his or her life, our global community must now tend to its worldwide problems and needs.

Looking at the social problems of the world in terms of the same hierarchy of needs we used to understand ourselves can help us better understand our world. When we feel our basic needs are threatened, it's hard to share and cooperate with others. But that cooperation is often exactly what's required to get everyone's needs filled.

Together, we can begin finding ways to meet the basic needs of all the earth's people. It really is within our collective power to resolve these issues now. We can solve the problems of poverty, hunger, health care, war and violence of all kinds, including the violence we perpetrate against the earth itself. We can create a world of safety and security for everyone. We can create a sense of belonging to the whole family of humanity. And we can begin reaching for the higher stars of self-actualization—a world that brings out the best in everyone and every group and allows their contributions to be made for the benefit of the whole world.

CARE, BELIEVE, AND TAKE ACTION

Religions, philosophies, and ideologies of all times and places have expressed the ideas of universality, global community, and other similar beliefs. *If we already know all of this, if people have been saying it for ages, then why aren't we living it yet?* I think what we need at this time to make our highest, wisest, and best hopes for humanity come true are three simple steps: We have to *care, believe,* and *take action.*

First, we need to feel that all of these global issues and problems have something to do with *us.* We have to understand that *we* are affected by shrinking tropical rainforests and growing holes in the ozone layer; by violence all over the world; by hunger, poverty, homelessness, and disease. This is largely a matter of education. If we take the time to learn about global issues in depth, we can't help but recognize our place in the human community and our global interconnectedness.

Second, we need to believe that positive change *can* happen, and *we* can help it to happen. Mei-Ying, who told us about her experiences in China and America when she was growing up, tells us that it is her strong idealism that has kept her going and happy for her nearly fifty years of life. She says, "I think you have to be capable of a little positive self-deception in this world."

Maybe it is more realistic to be cynical or pessimistic, giving up on politics, religion, philosophy, business, and people, in light of the horrors we see everywhere in the world. But we can also see signs of hope—if we look for them. We can remember a time when changes and circumstances we now take for granted were considered unrealistic dreams. We need ideals and myths that help us make sense of the world and lead us to the best possible choices. Idealism is a necessary underlying mythology for positive change to occur. We can create change and solve problems when we *believe* we can.

Finally, we must take our concern and our hope and turn them into *action*. Everything we do has effects in the world. We are all making a difference, all the time. What kind of difference are we making? How are we contributing to the new mythology, the new world? What small things can we do—as individuals and groups—to help solve the big problems and issues in our world?

Moving Forward

All these changes happening so quickly can seem confusing and frightening. Some of us retreat to our self-absorbed cynicism or dream of the good old days, when, we imagine, everything was better. But these viewpoints will neither help the needed changes occur, nor stop them from happening. It's impossible to move backward in time, and the "good old days" were never all that good, anyway. Nostalgic hindsight tends to blur our vision of the past. Tomorrow is what we have to create, and today is when we have to create it.

Viktor Frankl has said that we may have become so afraid of having values imposed upon us that we're against values altogether. But refusing to examine our mythologies, values, and choices only dooms us to living out a mishmash of old conflicting and self-defeating myths and values. We have it within our power to consciously choose our mythologies, values, and their resulting choices.

We can examine the underlying myths, values, and ideals that caused our current problems in the first place. If we take corrective actions without this examination, we'll only repeat our past mistakes over and over again. If we examine our mythology without turning our knowledge into new actions, we'll stay exactly where we are. Action or examination alone can't solve our problems now and for the future. But balance between examining our mythologies and consciously choosing new myths and actions can create the needed changes and guide us to our best possible future.

Now is the time to use all the wisdom humanity has managed to accumulate over the ages. The urgency to contribute is upon every one of us. As change occurs more and more rapidly, our values, ethics, and priorities, and our underlying sense of purpose and meaning are more and more important. What kind of future will we create? I don't know. But I do know the choice is ours. We can remain lost among the shadows that separate us, or we can find the one great vision to bring us together and light the path to our future.

Bibliography
And Suggested Reading

Augros, Robert M., and George N. Stanciu. *The New Story of Science*. Lake Bluff, Ill.: Regnery Gateway, 1984.

Baldwin, Christina. *Life's Companion*. New York: Bantam Books, 1991.

Berman, Phillip L. *The Search for Meaning: Americans Talk About What They Believe and Why*. New York: Ballantine Books, 1990.

Campbell, Joseph. *The Inner Reaches of Outer Space*. New York: Perennial Library, 1988.

Campbell, Joseph. *Myths To Live By*. New York: Bantam Books, 1973.

Campbell, Joseph with Bill Moyers. *The Power of Myth*. New York: Doubleday, 1988.

Capacchione, Lucia. *The Creative Journal*. Athens, Ohio: Swallow Press, 1989.

Capacchione, Lucia. *The Well-Being Journal*. North Hollywood, Calif.: Newcastle Publishing, 1989.

Elgin, Duane. *Voluntary Simplicity*. New York: William Morrow, 1981.

Erikson, Erik H. *Identity and the Life Cycle*. New York: W.W. Norton, 1980.

Erikson, Erik H. *The Life Cycle Completed*. New York: W.W. Norton, 1985.

Feinstein, David, and Stanley Krippner. *Personal Mythology*. Los Angeles: Jeremy P. Tarcher, 1988.

Ferguson, Marilyn. *The Aquarian Conspiracy*. Los Angeles: Jeremy P. Tarcher, 1987.

Ferguson, Marilyn, Wim Coleman and Pat Perrin. *PragMagic*. New York: Pocket Books, 1990.

Frankl, Viktor. *Man's Search for Meaning*. New York: Washington Square Press, 1985.

Frankl, Viktor. *The Will to Meaning*. New York: New American Library, 1988.

Hoff, Benjamin. *The Tao of Pooh*. New York: Penguin Books, 1983.

Jung, Carl G. *The Archetypes and the Collective Unconscious*. Princeton, N.J.: Princeton/Bollingen Paperbacks, 1980.

Jung, Carl G. *Memories, Dreams, Reflections*. New York: Vintage Books, 1989.

Keen, Sam. *Faces of the Enemy*. San Francisco: Harper & Row, 1986.

Keen, Sam, and Anne Valley-Fox. *Your Mythic Journey*. Los Angeles: Jeremy P. Tarcher, 1989.

Maslow, Abraham H. *Motivation and Personality*. New York: Harper & Row, 1987.

May, Rollo. *The Cry for Myth*. New York: W.W. Norton, 1991.

Peck, M. Scott. *The Road Less Traveled*. New York: Touchstone, 1978.

Rainer, Tristine. *The New Diary*. Los Angeles: Jeremy P. Tarcher, 1978.

Schumacher, E. F. *A Guide for the Perplexed*. New York: Harper & Row, 1978.

Solly, Richard, and Roseann Lloyd. *JourneyNotes*. Center City, Minn.: Hazelden Educational Materials, 1989.

Wakefield, Dan. *The Story of Your Life*. Boston: Beacon Press, 1990.

More reading for your growing consciousness . . .

Trusting Intuition
by Helene Lerner-Robbins

Trust yourself. You can have faith in your personal and spiritual progress. These innovative meditation books affirm that you are where you need to be in your life journey.

My Timing Is Always Right

There are no coincidences and no mistakes. You are in the right place in your life. Overcome worry and anxiety about the frustrations of daily situations. Discover the principles of *synchronicity* and why people, places, and things are as they should be—right now—in your life. 96 pp.
Order No. 5471

Embrace Change

When old ways no longer work and new behaviors feel uncomfortable, *Embrace Change*. These affirmations and meditations help you make the most of the day and focus on the future. Find renewed courage for making changes in your attitudes, ideas, projects, and relationships. 96 pp.
Order No. 5470

Green Spirituality
Reflections on Belonging to a World Beyond Myself
by Veronica Ray

When you wonder, "What am I becoming spiritual for?" read *Green Spirituality*. Veronica Ray's meditations place special emphasis on moving beyond personal growth. This beautiful book is about caring for the human community—considering "Myself and Others," "Myself and My Communities," and "Myself and the Earth." 128 pp.
Order No. 5184

For price and order information, or a free catalog, please call our Telephone Representatives.

HAZELDEN EDUCATIONAL MATERIALS

1-800-328-9000	1-612-257-4010	1-612-257-1331
(Toll Free. U.S., Canada, & the Virgin Islands)	(Outside the U.S. & Canada)	(FAX)

Pleasant Valley Road • P.O. Box 176 • Center City, MN 55012-0176

HAZELDEN EUROPE

P.O. Box 616 • Cork, Ireland
Telephone: Int'l Code+353-21-314318 • FAX: Int'l Code+353+21+961269

GRAND PRIX AT THE GLEN
Revised Edition

GRAND PRIX AT THE GLEN
Revised Edition

by Robert B. Jackson

illustrated with photographs

HENRY Z. WALCK, INC. / *NEW YORK*

The photographs on pages 49, 62 and 68 are by Bill Cox, Camera 3. The photograph on page 19 is by John Dowd, Camera 3. Other photographs are by the author.

LIBRARY OF CONGRESS CATALOGING IN PUBLICATION DATA   JACKSON, ROBERT B
GRAND PRIX AT THE GLEN. SUMMARY: A HISTORY OF GRAND PRIX RACING INCLUD-
ING THE CARS, DRIVERS, AND TEAMS, WITH A DETAILED ACCOUNT OF THE 1973
RACE AT WATKINS GLEN, NEW YORK.   1. GRAND PRIX RACING — HISTORY —
JUVENILE LITERATURE.   2. WATKINS GLEN GRAND PRIX RACE — JUVENILE LITERA-
TURE.   [1. GRAND PRIX RACING — HISTORY.   2. WATKINS GLEN GRAND PRIX RACE.
3. AUTOMOBILE RACING]   I. TITLE.   GV1029.15.J32 1974   796.7′2′0974781
73-19872   ISBN 0-8098-2097-8

Contents

1 / *The Place*

PERCHED on the southern end of Lake Seneca in the Finger Lakes region of New York, Watkins Glen is a small, sleepy resort village much of the year. The residents go quietly about their rural business while, in season, the tourists admire the Glen, a deep, rocky ravine that is cut by eighteen waterfalls. Summer visitors also stare at the tall towers of the salt wells dotting the shore of the long, narrow lake and often take leisurely tours of nearby wineries pressing the many grapes grown on the heights above Lake Seneca.

One exception to this gentle pace was the famous Watkins Glen rock concert of 1973 that attracted so much attention; but it was not the first such

The deep and rocky ravine of Watkins Glen State Park has been attracting tourists for one hundred years.

interruption. Little Watkins Glen had already become accustomed to periodic large crowds by then because a well-known road racing course is located a few miles southwest of the lake. When events are scheduled there, the village undergoes a dramatic change. Racing drivers, mechanics and enthusiastic spectators stream into town, expanding the tiny population up to sixty times. Franklin Street echoes to the rasping exhausts of hundreds of sports cars, and "No Vacancy" signs are posted in front of motels for miles around. Drug stores sell large amounts of film, there is endless race talk in crowded restaurants, and excitement runs high all over the area.

The people of Watkins Glen have had long experience with the stirring world of speed because on October 2, 1948, modern-day U.S. road racing got its start there. Fifteen sports cars roared through the streets in the original Watkins Glen Grand Prix, one of the first road races to be held in this country since before World War I. The 6.6-mile course started at the county courthouse, ran down Franklin Street, turned sharply into the hills back of town, crossed the state park in which the Glen is located, and then followed twisting country roads down into the village again. At one point the route crossed a railroad line, and special arrangements were needed to stop trains during the race. While most of the competing cars were British MG's, Frank Griswold, the winner, drove a ten-year-old Alfa Romeo coupe.

From this small beginning sports car racing grew rapidly in the United States. Several courses were established in other parts of the country; and race schedules, entry lists and attendance figures grew larger each season. Still, every fall the drivers and their fans came back to "The Glen" for the biggest race of the year.

After a serious accident during the Fifth Annual Grand Prix (1952), a second course was laid out on hilly roads four miles west of Watkins Glen. This second course, 4.6 miles around and almost square in shape, was used for only three years. While it was no longer necessary to stop trains during a race, many expensive repairs were needed to keep the country roads in racing condition and most of the drivers objected to the circuit as being too dangerous.

The present closed course, located in the same general area, was therefore built to be used only for road racing, and as a result is much safer for both drivers and spectators. The circuit was constructed in two stages, the 2.35-mile course that was opened in 1956 being enlarged to an even more challenging 3.38 miles in 1971. Over the years the Glen course has not only become a special favorite of U.S. road racing fans, it has also been improved to the point that it is now considered one of the world's best by racing experts.

Although the annual fall sports car race was called the Grand Prix in the early days at Watkins Glen, the title was not strictly accurate because sports car racing and Grand Prix competition are distinctly different forms of road racing. While both are held on twisting road courses instead of the oval tracks used by Indianapolis, stock and midget cars, Grand Prix automobiles bear little resemblance to sports cars. Sports cars are dual-purpose automobiles, theoretically useful for general transportation as well as racing; but GP cars are built only for racing. They are single-seater, open-wheeled, all-out road racing automobiles without fenders, headlights or passenger seats to slow them down. And because Grand Prix cars are the fastest class of such single-seaters, Grand Prix competition is the ultimate form of road racing.

Grand Prix racing began in France in 1906 (*Grand prix*, pronounced "grahn pree," is French for "great prize"), and the sport has been extremely popular in Europe ever since then. After sports car racing, also popular in Europe since the early days of the automobile, had become established in this country during the 1950's, U.S. race organizers decided to import Grand Prix racing as well. The first Grand Prix of the United States was held at Sebring, Florida, in 1959 and the second at Riverside, California, in 1960. Attendance was very small at both races, and neither was a financial success.

In the early fall of 1961 it seemed that the third U.S. GP would not be held. Any professional promoter could have obtained the race by posting expense money, but none was interested because of the failures in 1959 and 1960. Then some of the residents of Watkins Glen, recalling the tradition and popularity of their amateur sports car races, took a very large chance. They assumed responsibility for organizing the event, guaranteeing the expense money, and that October the Watkins Glen Grand Prix became a true Grand Prix for the first time. The race was a great success and the Grand Prix of the United States has been held annually at Watkins Glen since then, the crowds increasing and growing more enthusiastic with every running.

2 / *The Cars*

ON THE FIRST WEEKEND of October each fall, when mornings are frosty and the autumn coloring is at its brightest, followers of Grand Prix racing from all over the world swarm to the Glen. For the Grand Prix of the United States has become not only the most important race on the U.S. road racing schedule, it is now a major event on the international racing calendar as well.

Up to fifteen GP races are held in as many different countries annually to determine a World Champion Driver and the winner of the International Cup for Grand Prix Manufacturers. In 1973, for example, the championship series began at Buenos Aires, Argentina, in January and ended with the U.S. GP in October. Between were the Grands Prix of South Africa in March, Monaco in June, France in July, Germany in August and Italy in September. There were also championship races in Brazil, Spain, Belgium, Sweden, Great Britain, Holland, Austria and Canada, plus two additional non-championship races in Great Britain.

The overall GP list usually varies a bit from season to season, but in recent years the United States Grand Prix has been scheduled as the concluding race of the championship. And because the prize money at the U.S. GP is now the richest in road racing—$50,000 going to first place alone, more than four times the amount given any GP winner elsewhere—the Watkins Glen event customarily attracts the strongest field of all the Grands Prix. This is true even in those years that the championships have already been decided by October.

In common with the rest of international motor sport, Grand Prix racing is organized and controlled by the Federation Internationale de l'Automobile (FIA), whose headquarters is in Paris. The FIA determines the rules for all international competition of sedans, sports cars and single-seaters, sets up yearly schedules for their events, and licenses the drivers who race them.

Each of the several classes of FIA single-seaters is governed by a set of regulations called a "formula." Grand Prix automobiles, fastest and most prestigious of the formula cars, must be built according to Formula One and are therefore often called Formula One, or F1, cars. The smaller Formula Two and still smaller Formula Three cars which compete in many professional races throughout Europe are highly popular in their own right, too; and they often serve as training grounds for future Grand Prix drivers. (Technically, the term "Grand Prix" applies only to a championship Formula One race, but "Grand Prix" and "Formula One" are now used almost interchangeably.)

These formulas are periodically reviewed by the FIA to encourage technical advancement; and the current Formula One, in effect since 1966, is subject to change in 1976. A Grand Prix engine is now limited to twelve cylinders and a maximum size of three liters (183 cubic inches) unless it is supercharged to gain additional power. If a Formula One engine were to be equipped with a supercharger, which is a pump forcing additional gasoline-and-air mixture into the cylinders, it could be only half as large, 1.5 liters. This restriction on size is considered so severe by Grand Prix teams, however, that no supercharged cars have ever raced under the present Formula One.

Even though Grand Prix engines are relatively small and are also required to run on pump gasoline instead of the special fuel mixtures used by Indy and some drag cars, they are extremely powerful. From their 183-cubic-inch capacity most of them now crank out nearly five hundred horsepower, while in comparison the 350-cubic-inch engine of a Chevrolet Impala is rated at 160 horsepower.

Grand Prix engines can produce such vast power because they are built according to the most advanced designs from highest quality materials with super-precise hand construction. These are all steps that greatly increase their final cost as well as their top speed, though; and a Grand Prix engine is priced as high as $20,000 these days.

The production of so much horsepower, particularly for the size of the engine, also demands that each moving part be continually stressed just short of its theoretical limit. Consequently the reliability of Formula One engines is far less than that of street engines, which are relatively lightly stressed. In spite of being rebuilt after every race, the highly tuned GP engines often break down in use, and a two-car team therefore needs at least

The wheels have been removed from this Brabham BT42 and the Ford-Cosworth V-8 engine shows clearly. Note the big air scoop, the gearbox behind the rear axle and, to the rear of the gearbox, its oil radiator. An inboard brake disc can also be seen.

five of the expensive power plants for serious competition. During the 1973 season only the BRM and Ferrari teams built their own engines (twelve-cylinder types in both cases), all the other teams buying English Ford-Cosworth V-8's.

Grand Prix cars are feather-light to take full advantage of their strong engines. For one thing, they have monocoque bodies, rigid plastic or aluminum "tubs" that do not need heavy frames to support them. Also, the engine, which is located behind the driver for better weight distribution to improve the car's handling, has itself been made a load-carrying part of the main structure. A typical GP chassis ends just back of the cockpit, where the engine and gearbox are bolted to it, the rear suspension then being directly attached to the engine.

To make certain of reasonably solid construction, however, the current Formula One specifies that cars must weigh at least 575 kilograms, which is 1,265 pounds. In comparison a Chevrolet Impala, with approximately one-third the power of a GP car, weighs 4,435 pounds. In other words, a Grand Prix car has a power-to-weight ratio nearly twelve times that of an Impala.

The squat, wedgelike body of a representative Grand Prix car nestles between thirteen-inch wheels carrying fat tires that approach one foot in width at the front and a foot and a half in the rear. From a broad chisel-shaped nose that may have miniature wings extending on either side to keep it from lifting at high speed, the bodywork

*A Lotus 72D Grand Prix car, winner of the 1973 Constructors'
Championship.*

then sweeps upward to a tiny, cramped cockpit only
about two feet high at the top of its stubby horse-
shoe windshield.

In fact, Grand Prix cars are now so low and their
cockpits so small that the drivers must race lying
nearly flat upon their backs with just their helmeted
heads visible to the spectators. The drivers are also

forced to shift gears with only their right hands, there not being enough room to move their arms; and the stout, leather-covered steering wheels, to whose slightest movements the speeding cars instantly respond, are less than a foot across.

Water radiators for the engine are usually located on either side at the rear of the cockpit, well out in the cooling airstream, rather than at the front where they would increase the frontal area and cause greater air resistance. Grand Prix cars also have a high scoop mounted over the engine to force additional air into the fuel injection system and thus increase the engine's efficiency. In addition many have smaller scoops or ducts directing air to help cool their brakes.

Slung out at the back is the adjustable wing, pressing down with the weight of the air above it on the rear suspension and greatly increasing the car's adhesion to the road, particularly in the turns. Below the wing, attached to the rear of the gearbox, is the car's red warning light which must be turned on at the direction of race officials to slow following competitors in case of trouble.

Other safety equipment required by the FIA includes foam-filled rubber bladders to hold gasoline. Such fuel cells lessen the danger from fire;

and while the FIA permits Grand Prix cars a maximum of 250 liters (sixty-six gallons) of gasoline, the most that can be placed in any one cell is eighty liters (21.12 gallons). Furthermore, that area of the car containing fuel cells must be sheathed with a crushable structure of specified strength to protect the cells in case of a collision.

A built-in extinguisher system is necessary, too, as is a second braking system in case of failure of the first. A starter to get the car moving again in case it stalls, a rollbar projecting above the driver's head to protect him should the car turn over, and a six-point safety harness for the driver are also required.

To be competitive, GP drivers must continually push these cars to the very edge of losing control— "on the limit," they call it. If the fastest possible speed of a car through a particular turn without "losing it" is 110 miles an hour, its driver must do better than 109—but not exceed 110—lap after lap without making a mistake. The closer he can approach the "limit," the faster he will be.

A good driver is also aware of the changes in the maximum speed of a turn as the race progresses. Oil and rubber on the road may make it necessary to reduce speed or vary the "line" through a turn;

and the handling of the car may change as it becomes lighter with less gasoline in its tanks.

A racing driver seldom thinks in terms of miles per hour, and GP cars do not have speedometers. The most important dial on a Grand Prix instrument panel is a tachometer, which measures the speed at which the crankshaft of the engine is turning. The crankshaft is rotated by the pistons sliding up

The cockpit of an M23 McLaren. The tachometer is just behind the spoke of the small but stout steering wheel, and the stubby gear-shift lever is at the right.

and down in their cylinders, and then itself turns the rear wheels of the car through a series of parts called the power train. The number of revolutions per minute (rpm) of the crankshaft as shown by the needle of the tachometer is a more accurate measurement of an engine's performance than can be learned from a speedometer. Drivers are told the maximum rpm of an engine and are warned not to "rev" higher than this "red line," or the engine may "blow" (break). Many tachs have a second needle that remains at the highest rpm reached during a run. Called a "tell-tale" by the drivers because it shows how hard a car has been driven, it is not popular with them.

GP cars have five-speed gearboxes to gain the most power possible from their relatively small engines; and their drivers must constantly downshift and upshift as they enter curves and accelerate out of them. (Because GP gearboxes are located at the rear of the car operating directly upon the rear axle, they are more correctly called "transaxles" than "transmissions.") A driver refers to his speed through a turn by mentioning the gear he uses as well as his tachometer reading ("10,000 in fourth"), rather than miles per hour. To compare cars or drivers on an overall basis, lap times are used.

3 / *Teams and Drivers*

BECAUSE racing Formula One cars requires such great skill and judgment, there are only about two dozen drivers in the world at any one time capable of Grand Prix competition. Furthermore, only the top three or four of these two dozen are likely to be of championship ability.

After the beginning of Grand Prix racing in France in 1906, French, Italian and German teams dominated the sport for several decades. Since the late fifties, however, British cars and drivers have been the ones to beat in most seasons. The first British Grand Prix car to win the Constructors' Championship was the 1958 Vanwall; and Mike Hawthorn became the first British World Champion in the same year at the wheel of an Italian Ferrari.

By then the Cooper Car Company, a small British father-and-son racing organization, had begun its revolution of Grand Prix racing, also. In 1956, when the other GP teams were still fielding bulky front-engined automobiles, Charles and John Cooper had built the first of the low, light, mid-engined cars. The then-radical design was eventually copied by their competitors, but the Coopers' head start enabled them to win the Constructors' Championship in both 1959 and 1960.

Cooper's number-one driver and the World Champion in these years was Jack Brabham, an Australian. Brabham later left Cooper to build and race his own cars; and in 1966 he became the first driver to win the World Championship in a car of his own manufacture. The Cooper team dropped out of Grand Prix racing in 1969 and Jack Brabham has since retired as well, but Brabham cars are still being campaigned in Formula One. They have not been as successful in recent years as when "Black Jack" himself was in the cockpit, though. In 1973 the fastest Brabham driver was Carlos Reutemann, an Argentinian who improved greatly in only his second year of Grand Prix competition.

A British Grand Prix team with an even longer

history than Cooper or Brabham is BRM, British Racing Motors. Organized in 1945 with the financial help of several automobile-parts manufacturers, BRM first entered competition in 1950 and was purchased by the Owen industrial group in 1952. A familiar feature of GP starting grids for almost a quarter of a century, the BRM team has had more than its share of disappointments, its only championship coming in 1962 when Graham Hill won the drivers' title.

When Jack Brabham was number-one driver for Cooper, their number two was a young New Zealander, Bruce McLaren. At the end of his very first season with Cooper, Bruce won the inaugural Grand Prix of the United States, held at Sebring, Florida, in 1959. Then, when Jack Brabham left Cooper to form his own team, Bruce replaced him as the lead driver and later left Cooper himself to set up his own racing organization.

Thus far Bruce McLaren Racing, Ltd. has had its biggest successes with the big orange unlimited Can-Am sports cars that won nearly every race in the Canadian-American series for many seasons; and the group has also been very competitive in Indianapolis-type racing in the United States. Although the team has not done as well at Grand

Prix racing, the latest McLaren Formula One cars are much improved over earlier models and now run with the best.

Tragically, Bruce McLaren was killed while testing a new Can-Am car in 1970; and another New Zealander, Denny Hulme, who had been World Champion driving for Brabham in 1967 the

1973 McLaren drivers New Zealander Denny Hulme and American Peter Revson.

year before he joined the McLaren team, took over as the number-one McLaren driver in both the Can-Am and GP cars. A bluff, tough, balding veteran, Denny is often called "Big Bear" by the racing press.

Very few U.S. drivers have been active in Grand Prix racing to date, the only U.S. champion being Californian Phil Hill who won the title in 1961 driving for Ferrari. Many experts thought that Peter Revson, a member of the McLaren GP team in 1972 and 1973 might have become the second U.S. champion. But sadly, Peter, who drove a McLaren to the Can-Am championship in 1971 and was also a very successful Indy-type driver in McLaren cars, died in early 1974. Then on the Shadow team, he was practicing for the Grand Prix of South Africa when his suspension failed. (Other Americans on the McLaren team include Director Teddy Mayer, originally from Philadelphia, and Chief Engineer Tyler Alexander, who was born in Massachusetts.)

Driving a third car for Team McLaren in several of the 1973 Grands Prix was the controversial rookie, Jody Scheckter, a twenty-three-year-old South African. "Baby Bear" is recognized as one of the fastest new drivers to come along in many

Controversial 1973 newcomer Jody Scheckter, "Baby Bear."

seasons, but he also seems to be on the brink of disaster throughout every lap, sliding through each turn in an alarming fashion.

The third English driver to form his own Grand Prix team was John Surtees. The intense Surtees, seven times a world champion motorcycle racer before switching to automobiles, won the Grand Prix driving championship in 1964 when he was a member of the Ferrari team. He first raced a Formula One car of his own design in 1970, and since then he has gradually turned the actual driving over to others while he continues to direct the organization. His drivers in 1973 were rugged Mike "The Bike" Hailwood, who was also a British motorcycle racing star before he turned to cars, and Carlos Pace, a promisingly quick Brazilian.

Most experts agree the best driver of recent years has been Scot Jackie Stewart. Small and wiry, usually very talkative and always stylishly dressed, Jackie is widely popular, even among people who do not generally follow automobile racing. He began his single-seater racing with the Formula Three team of Ken Tyrrell, an English lumber dealer; and, in a most unusual step, advanced di-

Diminutive Scot Jackie Stewart, the best driver of recent years, retired in 1973.

rectly into Formula One competition with the BRM team shortly afterwards.

When Ken Tyrrell decided to enter Grand Prix racing in 1968, Jackie rejoined the team to drive one of Tyrrell's Matra Fords, French chassis with English engines. During 1969 Jackie swept six of the season's eleven Grands Prix in the Matra to become World Champion.

The following year Ken Tyrrell startled the racing world by suddenly unveiling his own Tyrrell GP car, designed and built with the greatest secrecy. And, after only a very short period of development for a Grand Prix automobile, the diminutive Jackie began winning again, taking his second World Championship, with the Tyrrell, in 1971.

By the U.S. GP of 1973 Jackie had won a total of twenty-seven Grands Prix, two more than the previous record set by fellow Scot Jimmy Clark, World Champion in 1963 and 1965 and previously considered by many to be the greatest driver of all time. As the crowds poured into Watkins Glen that fall, Jackie had also clinched his third championship two races earlier; and there was much talk he might soon retire.

The most successful of the British Grand Prix

teams (indeed, the most successful of all GP teams) is the Lotus organization of dapper Colin Chapman. Chapman, who also makes agile little Lotus sports cars for the street, is known for his technically advanced automobiles; and many ideas he was the first to use on his GP Lotuses have been quickly copied by his competitors.

The first Team Lotus Grand Prix victory came at Watkins Glen in 1961, and through the end of the 1973 season Lotus cars had won fifty-four World Championship races, more than any other make. During the thirteen-year period a Lotus driver won the World Championship in five seasons.

The Lotus World Champions have been Scot Jimmy Clark (1963, 1965), Briton Graham Hill (1968), Austrian Jochen Rindt (1970) and, in 1972, Brazilian Emerson Fittipaldi. When "Emmo" (named for Ralph Waldo Emerson) won his first Grand Prix, the U.S. GP of 1970, he was relatively unknown, causing one of the racing newspapers to ask in its headline, "Emerson who?" Two years later, however, at the age of twenty-five, he became the youngest driver ever to win the championship and everyone knew who he was. Emerson's older brother, Wilson (named for Woodrow Wilson), is also a Grand Prix driver and was a member of the

Young Brazilian Emerson Fittipaldi, World Champion in 1972.

Brabham team in 1973. Together they are ardent builders and fliers of radio-controlled model aircraft in their spare time.

Also driving for the Lotus Formula One team in 1973, his first year with Colin Chapman, was Ronnie Peterson, a tall, blond Swede. Five times a kart champion in his youth and European Formula Two champion in 1971, Ronnie lived up to this early promise in 1973 when he set the fastest practice-time in nine Grands Prix and won four.

Considering sports car victories as well as

Formula One wins, the glamorous Ferrari team still
has a numerical edge over the other road racing
teams; but the Italian organization has been slipping
on the Grand Prix circuits lately. Run by the legend-
ary Enzio Ferrari, a crusty individualist who never
attends a race, the team withdrew its blood-red cars
for part of the 1973 GP season because they were
so uncompetitive. Disappointed, their number-one
driver, Jacky Ickx of Belgium, left before the
schedule was completed. A brilliant driver who
has long been regarded of championship ability by

Popular Belgian star Jackie Ickx left Ferrari in 1973 and signed with Lotus for 1974.

most observers, the personable Ickx signed with the Lotus team after the season was over.

If there have not been very many U.S. Formula One drivers, there have been even fewer U.S. Formula One teams. Those that have tried to compete with the European organizations have not been very successful, either. In fact, no U.S. car won a Grand Prix between 1921, when Jimmy Murphy won the French Grand Prix in a Duesenberg, and 1967, when Dan Gurney was victorious in his Eagle at Spa, Belgium.

Gurney's Formula One operation had to be disbanded shortly afterwards for lack of financial support, and the U.S. was once again unrepresented on Grand Prix entry lists. Then, in 1973, the U.S.-based Shadow team, already known for its all-black Can-Am sports cars, stepped up to Grand Prix racing and fielded similarly colored Formula One automobiles with U.S. flags painted on their airscoops. Behind the wheel for the new entrant in its first season were Briton Jackie Oliver, the Can-Am Shadow driver, and George Follmer, a testy thirty-nine-year-old GP rookie from Cali-

U.S. driver George Follmer, member of the U.S. Shadow team.

fornia who was the 1972 Can-Am champion driving Roger Penske's Porsche 917.

Besides these "factory" organizations building and racing their own Formula One cars, the Grand Prix circus usually includes a number of private entries each season. These independents are generally unable to build their own cars, so they buy them from the "works" teams, who naturally keep the fastest models for themselves. Also, the independents usually do not have as much financial backing as the larger teams from sponsors such as gasoline or cigarette companies. Their drivers are therefore young men on the way up or older men no longer of the first rank; and independently entered cars are customarily found fairly well back on starting grids and finishing lists.

A new "privateer" for the 1973 season was Lord Alexander Hesketh, a chubby, very rich twenty-two-year-old Briton. Noted for his relaxed pre-race preparations, the chic girls in his pits, and a habit of passing around the most expensive champagne after every race, young Lord Hesketh purchased a March 731G from March Engineering of England for the campaign.

The March group had not been doing very well with its own team Formula One cars (although they

Independent British driver James Hunt was a Grand Prix rookie in 1973.

did win the 1973 European Formula Two Championship); and the Hesketh driver was to be the relatively inexperienced James Hunt, generally referred to as "Hunt the Shunt" around the garages because the English often call a collision a "shunt." All in all, the Hesketh effort was not taken very seriously at first, even for an independent team, seemingly not even by the Hesketh people themselves most of the time.

4 / *The Season*

THE 1973 Grand Prix season was an especially exciting one with close contention for the Drivers' Championship throughout most of the long fifteen-race schedule. At the beginning of the year Brazilian Emerson Fittipaldi won the Grands Prix of Argentina and Brazil in his Lotus, with the Tyrrell of Jackie Stewart third in Argentina and second in Brazil. Grand Prix drivers receive championship points on a 9-6-4-3-2-1 basis; and Fittipaldi, the 1972 champion, thus had an eight-point lead over Stewart, the 1971 champion, to start the 1973 campaign.

A local boy also did well in the South African Grand Prix in March. Jody Scheckter, whose only other Grand Prix had been at Watkins Glen the previous fall, surprised everyone with the third-fastest qualifying time, sharing the front row of the starting grid with McLaren teammate Denny Hulme and Emerson Fittipaldi. "Little Bear" even led the race for a time after "Big Bear" had to pit with tire trouble, but it was Jackie Stewart who knifed up through the field from a poor starting position to eventually win. Emerson finished third, giving him twenty-two points to Jackie's nineteen after three races.

A Fittipaldi victory in the Spanish Grand Prix widened this difference temporarily, but Jackie closed it again by winning in Belgium. Next on the Grand Prix calendar was the famous race through the streets of the Mediterranean resort of Monte Carlo; and the 1973 version proved to be a race-long duel between the quick Scot and the fast Brazilian. Jackie held on to win, although by only 1.3 seconds; and the points totals then stood at Fittipaldi, forty-one, Stewart, thirty-seven.

The glamorous Grand Prix of Monaco is the social highlight of the GP year, so it was altogether fitting that Hesketh Racing make its Grand Prix debut in Monte Carlo; and jovial Lord Hesketh set up headquarters on his big yacht in the harbor,

*Twenty-two-year-old Lord
Alexander Hesketh, whose
Grand Prix team made its
debut at Monaco in 1973.*

giving many parties there. James Hunt drove well
enough in the race itself, but the engine of his
March failed in the late laps, and the Hesketh entry
could not complete its first event.

The much-traveled Formula One set then
journeyed to Sweden for that country's initial Grand
Prix; and Swede Ronnie Peterson had his Lotus in
the lead with only two laps to go. A deflating tire
suddenly dropped him to a second-place finish
behind Denny Hulme, however; and Jackie
Stewart's fourth overall brought the Scot to within
only two points of Emerson Fittipaldi, who had
been forced to drop out by a broken gearbox.

The two rivals qualified on the front row of the grid for the French Grand Prix in July with the McLaren of surprising Jody Scheckter between the Lotus and the Tyrrell. In spite of its being only his third Grand Prix, the audacious Jody then outdragged everyone at the start and held first place in front of the closely pursuing Emerson Fittipaldi and Ronnie Peterson for most of the race. While Jody has a reputation for using so much of the road as to make passing him almost impossible, it was Emerson who made a mistake on the forty-second lap, trying to overtake where there was no room. The Lotus and the McLaren collided, putting both cars out of the race and assuring Ronnie Peterson the first Grand Prix victory of his career.

Jackie Stewart placed fourth in France and James Hunt was a creditable sixth, earning his first championship point. In 1973 the best seven results of the first eight races and the best six results of the last seven were counted toward the final championship totals; and by the "halfway" mark after the French Grand Prix Stewart had moved in front of Fittipaldi by the smallest possible margin, forty-two points to forty-one.

It had not been Jody Scheckter's error that had

taken him out of the lead in the French GP, but Jody finally did push his car past the limit in the British Grand Prix. While he was holding third place at the start of the second lap, he went into a difficult corner too quickly. The tail of his McLaren broke loose, and he spun directly in front of most of the field, knocking eight cars out of the race, including his own. Fortunately, only one driver was slightly injured, although the event had to be stopped and then restarted. The ultimate winner was McLaren driver and U.S. star, Peter Revson, only the sixth U.S. driver ever to have won a Grand Prix. James Hunt, improving with each race, took the checkered flag fourth.

Since neither Jackie nor Emerson had finished within the top six in Great Britain, they were still separated by a single point when they arrived in Holland for the tenth race of the series. In what was probably the turning point of the season, a wheel on Emerson's Lotus snapped during practice on the seaside course, and he crashed, jamming his right ankle. He had to withdraw from the race after only two laps because of the injury, and Jackie's victory moved him ahead in the championship struggle by a ten-point edge.

Third in Holland was James Hunt of Hesketh

Racing. By now no one seemed to be calling him "Hunt the Shunt" any longer; and because the Hesketh March had won eight championship points while the March factory team had been accumulating none, the low-pressure Hesketh group was receiving more and more attention.

Jackie won again on the twisting Nürburgring of Germany, and this meant that Emerson had to do well in Austria to stay in championship contention. Lotus teammate Ronnie Peterson did wave him by into the lead, but when a fuel line on the Fittipaldi car broke only a few laps from the end, Ronnie and Jackie swept past for a one-two finish.

With only three GP races left in 1973, a victory in the Italian Grand Prix was now essential to Emerson's fading championship chances. And when Ronnie and he were able to lead the pack in nose-to-tail order for much of the race and Jackie had to pit to change a tire, such a win for Emerson appeared entirely possible. Once Jackie was back on the course, however, he drove at his very best, breaking the lap record time after time as he continually improved his position.

Meanwhile, the Lotus pits had not given Ronnie the signal to move over that would have put Emerson into the lead for the three extra points to

Jackie Stewart, 1973 World Champion, at speed in his Tyrrell.

keep his title hopes alive. There had been increasing talk throughout much of the season that all was not well between Emerson and the Lotus organization, anyway, and this incident led many to conclude that Emerson would be driving for another team the following season. On the other hand, Stewart's teammate, Francois Cevert of France, allowed the brilliantly charging Jackie to pass him, and the first four finishers were Peterson, Fittipaldi, Revson and Stewart. Jackie now had sixty-nine points as compared to Emerson's forty-eight and was thus assured of his third World Championship.

The Canadian Grand Prix that followed was one of the most confusing GP races ever held. Run at Mosport Park, sixty miles east of Toronto, the start was delayed by heavy September rains; and later Jody Scheckter's McLaren and the Tyrrell of Francois Cevert tangled. The many pit stops to change from wet to dry tires and the restart from pace laps after the collision so confused the scoring that official results were not released until four hours after the race was over. Emerson Fittipaldi had driven into the victory circle, convinced he had won, but the official winner turned out to be Peter Revson, taking his second Grand Prix of the season.

Only the Grand Prix of the United States, richest race of the long, tough series now remained. And as the nights cooled and the leaves began to turn color, race preparations started to quicken the pace of life in little Watkins Glen.

5 / *Practice*

EXTENSIVE practice periods are held before each Grand Prix; and at Watkins Glen, where the race takes place on Sunday afternoon, Friday and Saturday are practice days. The spectators, many of whom pitch tents near favorite turns and combine attending the race with a camping trip, begin arriving as early as Wednesday. By Saturday morning the infield bristles with tents and campers, the smell of wood smoke is strong, and the fences are lined several deep with enthusiasts.

GP practice is held for three reasons: to determine starting positions for the race (the faster the practice times, the closer to the front of the starting grid); to familiarize the drivers with the course;

and, most important of all, to give the teams a chance to set up their cars for the circuit.

Many mechanical adjustments must be made to a GP car to gain maximum speed over a particular course. Springs, shock absorbers and tire pressures are matched to the surface of the road, the speed of the course and the direction of its bends. Fuel injectors are set according to the air temperature and altitude; and gearing is decided upon by the lengths of the straights as well as the sizes of the curves. And, because Grand Prix cars are continually being modified between races in a constant search for the tiniest fraction-of-a-second gain in lap speeds, these changes must also be tested.

At the Glen in 1973 there was a hard rain on Thursday night; but by the time the course was opened for practice Friday morning, a bright sun was reflecting from Lake Seneca and the autumn foliage of its surrounding hills. The first car to leave the pits was the scarlet-and-white BRM of Austrian Niki Lauda, followed by the blue-and-white Surtees of Mike Hailwood, the yellow March of Mike Beuttler, and Carlos Reutemann's white Brabham. Circulating relatively slowly at first, they stopped at their pits every few laps for adjustments.

Soon they were gradually joined by the other

Mike Hailwood and the Surtees crew prepare for practice.

entries, including orange-and-white McLarens, black-and-gold Lotus's, blue Tyrrells and a red Ferrari. In addition to its colorful paint job each car carried several advertisements for the companies sponsoring the team, with the exception of the white March of Lord Hesketh. He is wealthy enough to spurn the financial support of commercialism, and his car was marked only by red and blue stripes across the cockpit area, without a decal in sight.

As the number of cars speeding around the course increased, fans along the fences checked the number of each newly appearing car against their programs for identification. Many of the more enthusiastic also made mental note of the helmet colors of their favorite drivers for quick recognition later on. As examples, Peter Revson's was white with a red-and-blue pattern on its sides; Ronnie Peterson wore a blue one with a yellow visor; and Jackie Stewart's white helmet was circled with a band of the family tartan.

Most U.S. spectators were particularly waiting to see the U.S.-sponsored Shadow team. Like nearly all beginning Grand Prix efforts, the new group had been having difficulties in making its cars competitive. Still, George Follmer had finished third in Spain, and Jackie Oliver had placed third in Canada. Also, the team had been strengthened for Watkins Glen by the addition of a third jet-black car for British driver Brian Redman.

George Follmer, who finished third in the Spanish Grand Prix, during practice at Watkins Glen in his Shadow.

Then there was the independently entered white Shadow of long-time Glen favorite Graham Hill, a Briton in his nineteenth year of automobile racing. The dashing, witty Hill won the U.S. GP in 1963, 1964 and 1965, was World Champion with BRM in 1962 and Lotus in 1968, and has also been victorious at both Le Mans and Indianapolis. Now regarded as the "Elder Statesman" of Grand Prix competition, he is usually found farther back on starting grids than in his earlier years.

The Grand Prix qualifying record at Watkins Glen, set by Jackie Stewart in 1972, stood at one minute, 40.481 seconds as Friday's practice began. This represents an average speed of 120.991 mph, and maintaining such an average through the eleven tricky turns of the 3.377-mile course requires a top speed of nearly one hundred and eighty miles per hour on the fastest straight.

Once the four-hour practice session was under way, the surface of the road dried from the night's rain, the mechanics systematically improved the tune of the cars, and the drivers became faster and faster. A strong wind did hold speeds down a bit, but Ronnie Peterson in his Lotus came within eleven-thousandths of a second of Jackie's record and set Friday's best time, 1:40.492. Jackie himself was second fastest (1:40.635), and Jackie's Tyrrell teammate, Francois Cevert, winner of the U.S. GP in 1971, was the third-fastest (1:41.044).

Grand Prix mechanics must often work exhaustingly long hours under difficult conditions, and Friday night was such a time for many of them. The engines of Jackie Oliver's Shadow and Niki

Grand Prix mechanics must work long hours on race weekends. These are checking a BRM P160.

Lauda's BRM needed to be changed, for instance, and all three BRM's got new gears overnight. Also, the wing, bodywork, suspension and radiator on the left side of Graham Hill's Shadow had to be replaced because he had struck a steel retaining barrier when his suspension broke at speed.

James Hunt in the Hesketh March was sixteenth fastest (1:43.834) on the first day of practice, primarily because the car was sluggish in responding to steering. Therefore the Hesketh team was busy late on Friday night, too, fitting a different nose section to the March in an attempt to improve the handling.

The weather on Saturday was clear and warm once again; and the steadily growing crowd was pleased to learn that, in a surprise move, the popular ex-Ferrari driver Jackie Ickx had arrived to take over the second car of Frank Williams' Iso team. He was not to have much success with his new ride at first, however, qualifying twenty-third.

As usually happens on the second day of practice when the weather holds, most teams improved their lap times. By the second hour speeds had increased to the point that four drivers had already broken the 1972 qualifying record. Fastest was Ronnie Peterson (1:39.657 or 121.99 mph), then came Brabham driver Carlos Reutemann (with a surprising 1:40.013), Emerson Fittipaldi (1:40.393) and Francois Cevert (1:40.444).

Just as the morning practice session was coming to a close, Francois Cevert attempted to better his probable fourth-place starting position, and tragedy struck. Streaking through the Esses on the uphill part of the course, his Tyrrell suddenly fishtailed.

The car hit the steel guardrails on the outer side of the road, bounced across to the inner barrier, and, then completely out of control, slammed back through the outer rails, killing its driver instantly.

Shocked and stunned, few drivers improved their positions in the final afternoon hour of practice. The Tyrrell team withdrew from the next day's race in respect for its French star; and there was much quiet talk about his accident around the campfires and in the motels that evening.

6 / *The Race*

RACE DAY dawned brisk and overcast. Before long campers all around the circuit were struggling out of sleeping bags and starting breakfast fires in front of their tents, while the first drowsy spectators appeared to stake out favorite viewing spots along the fences and in the stands. Although the race would not start until two-thirty in the afternoon, the narrow country lanes leading to the course gradually jammed with thousands of cars; and by noon traffic was backed up for several miles into Watkins Glen itself. Those who had not already left town were not likely to see the start.

During the morning many enthusiasts trudged around the course to see what it was like first-hand,

and later there was an exciting free-fall demonstration by Navy parachutists trailing colored smoke across the clearing sky. About noon a group of vintage sports and racing cars that had run a short race after practice on Saturday made a two-lap tour of the circuit. Then came a parade of the Grand Prix drivers as passengers in open Corvettes.

Interesting as these preliminaries were, everyone was concentrating upon the race to come, and

On the morning of the U.S. GP many enthusiasts walk the course to see what it is like firsthand. In 1973 the mud they left behind affected the start of the race.

Starting grid, 1973 U.S. GP. Car numbers, drivers, drivers' countries, cars and best practice times.

10. Carlos Reutemann
Argentina
Brabham BT42
1:40.013

2. Ronnie Peterson
Sweden
Lotus 72D
1:39.657

27. James Hunt
England
March 731G
1:40.520

1. Emerson Fittipaldi
Brazil
Lotus 72D
1:40.393

23. Mike Hailwood
England
Surtees TS14
1:40.844

5. Jackie Stewart
Scotland
Tyrrell 006
1:40.635 **WITHDRAWN**

7. Denis Hulme
New Zealand
McLaren M23
1:40.907

8. Peter Revson
USA
McLaren M23
1:40.895

0. Jody Scheckter
South Africa
McLaren M23
1:41.321

24. Carlos Pace
Brazil
Surtees TS14
1:41.125

29. Chris Amon
England
Tyrrell 005
1:41.679 **WITHDRAWN**

4. Arturo Merzario
Italy
Ferrari 312B3
1:41.455

20 Jean-Pierre Beltoise
France
BRM P160
1:42.417

31. Brian Redman
England
Shadow DN1
1:42.247

#30. Jochen Mass
Germany
Surtees TS14
1:42.517

#12. Graham Hill
England
Shadow DN1
1:42.848

#16. George Follmer
USA
Shadow DN1
1:43.387

#17. Jackie Oliver
England
Shadow DN1
1:43.650

#9. John Watson
N. Ireland
Brabham BT42
1:43.887

#15. Mike Beuttler
England
March 731
1:45.032

#19. Clay Regazzoni
Switzerland
BRM P160
1:42.468

#18. Jean-Pierre Jarier
France
March 731
1:42.752

#25. Howden Ganley
New Zealand
Iso IR
1:43.166

#21. Niki Lauda
Austria
BRM P160
1:43.543

#26. Jacky Ickx
Belgium
Iso IR
1:43.885

#11. Wilson Fittipaldi
Brazil
Brabham BT 42
1:44.478

#28. Rikky von Opel
Lichtenstein
Ensign MN01
1:45.441

the suspense increased with each minute that passed. After the cars were finally pushed to the start-finish line for warm-up laps, most of the crowd came to its feet in anticipation as, one by one, the competitors began to wail about the circuit, the rhythm of their downshifts and upshifts resounding from the slopes of red and gold. As their favorites sped by, the spectators cheered them on, the appearance of Emerson Fittipaldi causing a frantic flourishing of Brazilian flags in the stands just across from the pits, for instance.

The excitement and tension mounted further as the twenty-five cars returned to the starting grid. The fastest qualifier, Ronnie Peterson's Lotus had the inside position of the first row, with the second-fastest, the Brabham of Carlos Reutemann, beside him. In the second row were the Lotus of Emerson Fittipaldi and the surprising Hesketh March, James Hunt having dramatically improved his best lap-time by more than three seconds on Saturday.

Jackie Stewart had been fifth fastest before withdrawing, and Mike Hailwood was sixth in the Surtees. Seventh was Peter Revson, teammate Denny Hulme was eighth, Carlos Pace qualified ninth in another Surtees, and Jody Scheckter was tenth. Brian Redman was the fastest of the four Shadow drivers, but even so, qualified his car back in the seventh row in thirteenth starting position.

Mechanics in spotless race-day coveralls made last-minute checks as clusters of photographers hovered about and team managers reviewed race strategy with their drivers. Five minutes before the start a warning cannon was fired, and four minutes later a second shot came as a signal to clear the grid of all but the competitors.

Engines roared fiercely as the ten-second sign was held high at the front of the grid and starter Tex Hopkins prepared to begin the race. He stood on a platform built above the pit rail, facing the noisy grid with the starting flag held high, wearing his usual lavender-colored suit, his customary big cigar jutting out of his mouth. Nearly everyone held his breath when Tex turned his back on the grid and stepped slowly away, checking his wristwatch. Suddenly, he jumped high in the air, lowering the flag as he spun toward the grid. Engines thundered, dust flew, and the screaming cars leaped forward. The fifteenth Grand Prix of the United States had started.

For all but the stationary Peter Revson, that is. His clutch partially failed, and, throwing his left arm

Engines thundering, the cars leap forward to start the fifteenth Grand Prix of the United States.

in the air to warn those behind him, he shifted into neutral. Once the other cars had swerved past, he banged his McLaren into gear and finally blasted away, dead last and knowing that he would have trouble on each of the many more gear changes to come on every lap.

Meanwhile the rest of the field had howled into the difficult ninety-degree right-hand turn at the end of the pit straight, where two more drivers encountered trouble. Spectators had tracked mud onto the course in the morning, and the mud had dried to become dust. This dust swirled up at the start and stuck the throttle slides of Brian Redman's Shadow and Rikky von Opel's new Ensign, putting both cars out of the race on only the first of its fifty-nine laps.

First away from the grid and leading the charging pack into the Ninety had been Ronnie Peterson with Carlos Reutemann and James Hunt close behind. Storming along the short straight at the northern end of the course, they swept uphill through the twisting Esses onto the long front straight, fastest part of the circuit, and into the Loop. Four more testing turns in the Anvil followed by a fast left-hander, then a bend to the right, and they were flashing down the pit straight again to complete their first lap. The three leaders maintained their positions, Emerson Fittipaldi was fourth, Mike Hailwood fifth, Denny Hulme sixth and Jody Scheckter seventh.

Much to the amazement of the crowd, the little-publicized James Hunt held third for two more laps; and on the fourth he even squeezed past Reutemann into second. By now Emerson Fittipaldi was experiencing handling difficulties and had dropped back to seventh.

On the next lap Mike Hailwood started losing

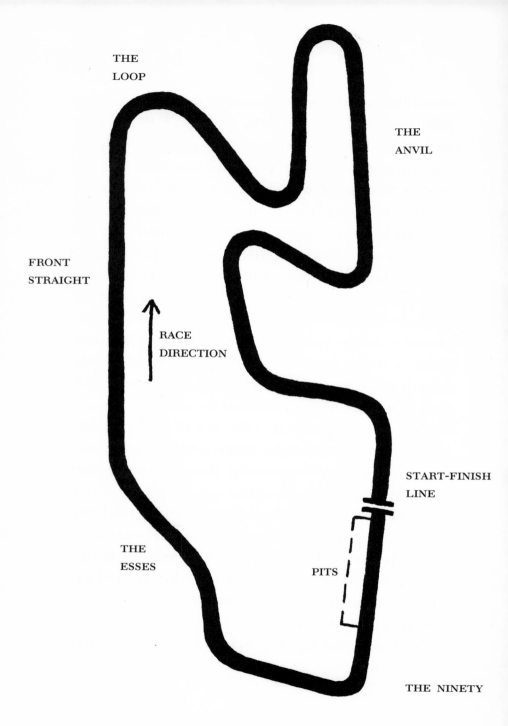

THE
LOOP

THE
ANVIL

FRONT
STRAIGHT

RACE
DIRECTION

START-FINISH
LINE

THE
ESSES

PITS

THE NINETY

WATKINS GLEN CIRCUIT, 3.377 MILES

ground because of a faulty rear suspension, Denny and Jody pushing past the Surtees to take over fourth and fifth positions. At the rear of the field their teammate, Peter Revson, was driving extremely well and moving steadily up the lap charts. Double-clutching all the way, at the end of the fifth lap he was eighteenth, on the eighth lap he was sixteenth, and by the twelfth lap he was fourteenth, having moved up eleven places.

The other U.S. driver, George Follmer, was not doing nearly as well, because the Shadow team, having already lost its fastest car, was running pretty much at the back of the action. Jackie Oliver passed Follmer on the eleventh lap for sixteenth place, but on the twenty-eighth he was himself passed by the independent Shadow of Graham Hill.

Meanwhile, the tight battle at the front of the field had the fans waving and shouting. Try as he might, Ronnie Peterson could not draw away from James Hunt; and the white March clung to the tail of the black-and-gold Lotus lap after lap. Reutemann chased them for third, and he was himself being pushed by fourth-place Hulme and fifth-place Scheckter. Fittipaldi was sixth and Peter Revson was already up to tenth.

Just past the halfway mark of the race, as the

/ 65

Try as he might, Ronnie Peterson (Lotus #2) could not draw away from James Hunt (March #27).

Lotus and the March were overtaking other cars in the Ninety, Peterson slid a bit in the dust and Hunt pulled even. Through the turn they came, side by side, nose to nose; and the crowd exploded into a frenzied uproar. As the pair accelerated on to the short straight, it was the Lotus that spurted ahead.

"I decided to back off and not try to pass," Hunt said later. "He looked fiercer than me." (Hunt, who wears his hair long and often smiles mischievously as he talks, was driving with the toes of his shoes cut off to give his feet greater clearance under a cross-brace of the cockpit.)

On the fortieth lap, with nineteen laps left to run, part of the rear suspension of Jody Scheckter's fifth-place McLaren snapped as he gunned out of the same turn; and he skidded to the side of the road, his race over. Just behind Jody, Emerson Fittipaldi had to brake so hard avoiding him that he wore his front tires to the fabric in one spot and was forced to pit for replacements. These developments moved the surging Peter Revson up to fifth, Fittipaldi dropping to sixth when he resumed competition.

The split-second battle for the lead still raged going into the final laps of the contest. One mistake on Peterson's part and Hunt would have taken over, but the Swedish ace continued to drive smoothly and skillfully in spite of the pressure behind him. Then, after trailing the Lotus for almost an hour and a half, Hunt did his utmost in the last five laps. Closer and closer he drew, cutting the difference to less than a second, turning the fastest lap of the race (one minute, 41.652 seconds — 119.596 mph) on the next-to-last circuit. It was not quite enough, however, and Peterson took the waving checkered

*Ronnie Peterson and Lotus Chairman Colin Chapman share the
1973 U.S. GP winner's cup.*

flag of leaping Tex Hopkins just .668 of a second
ahead of Hunt for his fourth Grand Prix victory of
1973.

Carlos Reutemann was a solid third, Denny
Hulme fourth, Peter Revson fifth after his splendid
drive from last, and Emerson Fittipaldi sixth.
Seventh, in another fine performance after starting
twenty-third in an uncompetitive Iso, was Jackie
Ickx.

Most of the morning had been needed to funnel spectators' cars into the course, but this traffic jam was slight compared to the tangle that resulted when more than 100,000 fans tried to leave after the race. All routes leading from the course were snarled for hours with thousands of crawling cars, and many enthusiasts with foresight did not plan to leave until later in the evening when traffic had thinned.

As the departing crowds milled about them, these old hands started their campfires for dinner, leaned back, and talked about the race and the long season that it had concluded, as well as the season to come. It had been a year of transition and re-alignment, and the Watkins Glen event had re-flected these changes.

Jackie Stewart, Grand Prix racing's best driver and spokesman for a number of seasons was about to retire, and new contenders for his place both on and off the track were emerging. Ken Tyrrell had already signed Jody Scheckter to drive for him in the coming year, for instance.

Also, Emerson Fittipaldi, who finished second to Jackie in the 1973 Drivers' Championship, was said to be leaving Lotus, winner of the Constructors' Championship in 1973, for the McLaren team; and

Jacky Ickx signed with Colin Chapman later that month. This meant that both Ronnie Peterson, third in the 1973 championship standings, and Jacky Ickx, regarded by many as second in ability only to Jackie Stewart, would be drivers for the most successful of Grand Prix teams, and either one could well be the next World Champion.

Winner of the U.S. GP and third in the championship standings in 1973, Ronnie Peterson is a likely champion of the future.

Demonstrating how quickly the highly competitive world of Grand Prix racing changes, it had only been one year since "Superswede" Ronnie had suffered through a drab season driving a team March. And, as further evidence, James Hunt had already arisen to challenge Ronnie, coincidentally in another March.

U.S. fans were particularly interested in the prospects for U.S. Grand Prix teams, of course. They expected that the Shadow team would improve after the experience of its first year. Dan Gurney, who had built the last U.S. car to win a Grand Prix (1967) was known to be working on a new Formula One Eagle, as well. There was also speculation that Roger Penske, widely known as the supremely successful team owner-manager of everything from Can-Am sports cars to NASCAR stockers, was considering entering Grand Prix racing on a regular basis. And the Indianapolis-style racing team of Parnelli Jones was thinking seriously of fielding a Grand Prix car for oval star Mario Andretti, winner of the 1971 South African Grand Prix in a Ferrari.

Road racing enthusiasts in the U.S. were fervently hoping these possibilities would materialize.

Then their dream of a U.S. driver's winning the Grand Prix of the United States in the cockpit of a car built in the United States might at last be fulfilled.